New HONEY & YOGURT Recipes

Rena Cross

Edited by Anne Gains

W. Foulsham & Co. Ltd.
London · New York · Toronto · Cape Town · Sydney

W. Foulsham & Company Limited
Yeovil Road, Slough, Berkshire, SL1 4JH

ISBN 0–572–01441–4
Originally published as The Honey and Yogurt Cookbook
in 1974. This completely revised and updated edition
Copyright © 1988 W. Foulsham & Co. Ltd.

Printed in Great Britain at St Edmundsbury
Press, Bury St. Edmunds.

CONTENTS

INTRODUCTION

Honey and yogurt are two natural foods which provide an extraordinary number of health benefits and for which, happily, there are no artificial substitutes. We all enjoy a little bit of honey on our bread and butter, and yogurt, too, has become a familiar part of our everyday diet. They have both played an important rôle in the natural way of life of places like Greece, Turkey, Egypt and India for thousands of years.

These days, honeys and yogurts of all sorts abound on supermarket and health-shop shelves. You can find fruit yogurts of every flavour as well as those that are especially low fat or extra creamy. They make delicious fruity snacks or desserts on their own but many contain additives such as extra sugar, cream or colouring, so when it comes to healthy cooking it is best to choose the most natural, plain yogurt or, best of all, to make your own so you know it contains none but the most natural ingredients.

You will find the shops full of a rich variety of honeys from all over the world. Look for those labelled 'pure' as blended honeys may contain sugar, syrup or other additives. Flavours vary widely but they all make much healthier and more natural sweeteners than refined sugars. For a start, honey is twice as sweet as sugar so you only need half as much!

The recipes in this book illustrate the countless ways in which yogurt and honey can be used in a healthy style of cooking. When you're in a hurry, though, and need a quick revitalizing snack, there's nothing more refreshing and delicious than a simple bowl of plain yogurt with some honey stirred in.

HONEY

Honey is a much-loved natural food that has been revered throughout history as much for its medicinal properties as for its nutritional value and flavour.

Honeys vary a great deal in taste depending on their region of origin and the type of flowers from which the bees gathered the nectar. The most readily available honeys include clover and heather, while 'speciality' honeys are those made from rose or lavendar nectar. These honeys not only have a taste of the particular flowers but also carry a hint of their fragrance.

Honey is produced in all parts of the world. Orange blossom honey comes from California. Australian honey is strong and almost always carries a tang of eucalyptus from the gum tree flowers.

The nectar collected by the honey-bee consists of sugars and water. It is carried from flower to hive in the bee's honey stomach. The enzymes inside the stomach convert sucrose in the nectar into the pre-digested sugars levulose and dextrose. This process continues after the nectar has been deposited in the honeycomb of the hive and moisture is evaporated off. Finally, when the honey is 'ripe', the worker bees cap it with wax.

As a result of this pre-digesting process, honey is very easily absorbed by our bodies. It passes quickly into the bloodstream to release heat and energy. Other forms of sugar need slower and more complicated digestion. Honey is the best sweetener to use for babies and young children because of this easy and rapid digestion, and it is better tolerated and assimilated than other sugars.

Honey is rich in vitamins, containing vitamins B_1 (thiamin), B_2 (riboflavin), B_3 (pantothenic acid), B_6, biotin and folic acid and vitamin C. It also contains the minerals iron, copper, sodium, potassium, manganese, calcium, magnesium and phosphorus. Obviously, these constituents vary from one type of honey to another, but it is believed that the darker honeys are the most concentrated nutritionally. Honey is said to have relaxing properties if drunk in hot milk at bedtime, and it is very commonly used in a hot drink with lemon to relieve cold symptoms. It is considered a gentle and natural laxative and is believed to aid blood-clotting, the healing of burns and the metabolism of fat. All in all, honey really is a wonder-food!

If stored correctly, honey will keep almost indefinitely. It has been found in perfect condition in a 3,300-year-old Egyptian tomb! Keep it, covered, in glass or stone containers in a cool place. If clear honey becomes crystallized on keeping, simply warm it gently and it will become clear again. When using honey in cooking, remember that its sweetening powers are greater than other sugars so you will need to use less.

YOGURT

Yogurt has been with us as long as there has been milk to turn sour. Milk has always been an important food but it does not stay fresh for very long. In hot weather, without refrigeration, milk soon turns sour but need not be wasted as it can be eaten as yogurt.

As milk goes sour and turns to yogurt it develops natural bacteria called *lactobacillus bulgaricus*. This has positive health benefits for us as this natural bacteria fights undesirable bacilli in our own digestive systems. Yogurt is more easily digested than milk and is absorbed faster, so it is an important food for invalids and for pregnant women who need extra calcium.

Yogurt is also recommended by some enlightened doctors to counteract the effects of taking anti-biotics. It is believed that anti-biotic drugs not only kill off the 'bad' illness-causing bacteria but also destroy the 'good' bacteria found in the intestine which are necessary to health. Antibiotics also cause a deficiency of B vitamins and yogurt bacteria are able to manufacture B vitamins in the intestine. It is essential that yogurt used for these purposes is 'live' yogurt, that is yogurt that has not been 'heat treated' which destroys the natural bacteria.

Making Your Own Yogurt
Making your own yogurt is not only quick, simple and very economical, but it also allows you to choose exactly which milk to use and how creamy or low-fat to make it. There

are many attractive yogurt makers on the market or you can simply use a wide-necked Thermos flask.

First, choose which milk you want to use. Cows' milk (whole or semi-skimmed) is probably the most commonly used, but you might also like to try sheep's, goats' or soya milk. If you like a thicker, creamier yogurt add 1 tablespoon skimmed milk powder.

Secondly, you will need a 'starter'. This can be either 1 tablespoon plain 'live' yogurt (not heat treated yogurt which has its beneficial bacteria killed by heat), or a commercial 'starter' *Lactobacillus bulgaricus*, usually in crystal form.

BASIC YOGURT RECIPE

Makes about 600 ml/1 pint/2½ cups

	Metric	Imperial	American
Milk	*600 ml*	*1 pint*	*2½ cups*
Plain 'live' yogurt or commercial yogurt starter crystals	*1 tbsp*	*1 tbsp*	*1 tbsp*
Skimmed milk powder (optional)	*1 tbsp*	*1 tbsp*	*1 tbsp*

1. Bring the milk to the boil in a saucepan and cool to 110°F/50°C (that is until you can comfortably hold a clean finger in the milk for a few seconds).

2. Mix a little cooled milk with the starter and the powdered milk, if using. Mix well and stir in the

remaining milk. Pour into yogurt maker cups or a Thermos flask and leave for at least 8 hours until set.

3. Keep 1 tbsp yogurt to use as a starter for your next batch. The yogurt will keep in the refrigerator for up to a week.

FRUIT AND NUT YOGURTS

Home-made fruit or nut yogurt can be made with virtually any fruit or nuts. Fruits such as raspberries may be used whole but others, such as peaches, are best chopped. Nuts, such as hazelnuts, should be finely chopped. The fruit or nuts should be added to the yogurt maker cups or flask before the boiled milk and starter mixture is poured in (see above). It is also possible to add them after the yogurt has set, but it is better to whip the yogurt until it is fluffy and then fold in the fruit or nuts. This can also be done in a blender or food processor but the resulting yogurt will not contain any whole pieces of fruit. Fruit yogurt can be sweetened with honey, if liked.

YOGURT CHEESE

Yogurt cheese is easy to produce and is an excellent low-fat substitute for cream cheese in many recipes. It is not unlike cottage cheese.

Simply line a sieve (strainer) with a double layer of clean muslin (cheesecloth). Place over a bowl, tip the yogurt into the prepared sieve and leave until enough whey has dripped through and the cheese is the consistency you require. Obviously, the longer it is left, the drier the cheese

11

becomes. (The whey can be used in drinks, sauces, soups or casseroles.)

Use yogurt cheese in a variety of recipes or flavour it with garlic, herbs, mustard, tomato purée (paste), etc., or with fruit purées for a cheesecake or dessert.

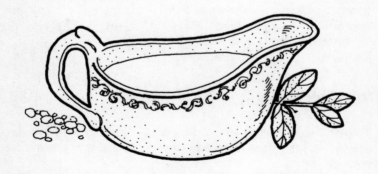

1
SAUCES, DRESSINGS AND DIPS

SAUCE TARTARE

Makes about 300 ml/½ pint/1¼ cups

	Metric	Imperial	American
Plain yogurt	250 ml	8 fl oz	1 cup
Lemon juice	1 tsp	1 tsp	1 tsp
Chopped fresh parsley	1 tbsp	1 tbsp	1 tbsp
Chopped green pepper	1 tbsp	1 tbsp	1 tbsp
Chopped capers	1 tbsp	1 tbsp	1 tbsp
Chopped chives	1 tsp	1 tsp	1 tsp
Celery seeds	1 tsp	1 tsp	1 tsp

1. Mix all the ingredients well, cover and leave in the refrigerator for the flavours to develop for several hours.

2. Serve with fish or vegetables, as a dip or with salads.

BÉCHAMEL (WHITE) SAUCE

Makes about 450 ml/¾ pint/2 cups

	Metric	Imperial	American
Milk	300 ml	½ pint	1¼ cups
Shallot or small onion, chopped	1	1	1
Blade of mace			
Bay leaf	1	1	1
Salt and pepper			
Margarine	40 g	1½ oz	3 tbsp
Plain (all-purpose) flour	25 g	1 oz	¼ cup
Plain yogurt	120 ml	4 fl oz	½ cup

1. Place the milk in a small saucepan. Add the shallot or onion, mace, bay leaf and seasoning and bring to the boil. Remove from the heat and leave to infuse for about 15 minutes.

2. Melt the margarine in a saucepan, add the flour and stir to make a roux. Cook for 1–2 minutes, stirring. Remove from the heat and gradually strain in the milk, stirring continuously. Bring to the boil and cook, stirring, until smooth and thickened. Taste and adjust the seasoning, then add the yogurt.

3. Serve with fish, vegetables or poultry, or use as a base for other sauces and dishes.

SAUCE BÉARNAISE

Makes about 450 ml/¾ pint/2 cups

	Metric	Imperial	American
Tarragon vinegar	100 ml	4 fl oz	½ cup
Shallot, chopped	1	1	1
Sprig of fresh tarragon			
Salt and pepper			
Egg yolks, lightly beaten	3	3	3
Plain yogurt	250 ml	8 fl oz	1 cup
Chopped fresh parsley	1 tsp	1 tsp	1 tsp

1. Combine the vinegar, shallot and tarragon in a saucepan. Season with salt and pepper and boil rapidly until reduced by about half. Cool and strain, reserving the tarragon.

2. Tear the leaves from the tarragon sprig and chop finely.

3. Place the vinegar in the top of a double boiler and heat gently without allowing the water in the bottom to boil.

4. Gradually beat the egg yolks into the vinegar and continue beating until the mixture thickens.

5. Add the yogurt, beating continuously, then remove from the heat and add the tarragon and parsley.

6. Serve immediately with steak or chops.

BARBECUE SAUCE

Makes about 600 ml/1 pint/2½ cups

	Metric	Imperial	American
Small onion, finely chopped	1	1	1
Olive oil	2 tbsp	2 tbsp	2 tbsp
Plain yogurt	250 ml	8 fl oz	1 cup
Worcestershire sauce	2 tbsp	2 tbsp	2 tbsp
Garlic clove, crushed	1	1	1
Tomato ketchup	250 ml	8 fl oz	1 cup
Chilli sauce (see note)			

1. Place all the ingredients in a saucepan, adding a few drops of chilli sauce to taste. Bring slowly to the boil and simmer for 10 minutes, stirring continuously.

2. Brush the sauce over meat while cooking on a barbecue or grill (broiler).

Note
To make chilli sauce, tightly pack a jar or bottle with dried chillies. (Ideally, use a jar or bottle with a 'shaker' screw top, such as a Worcestershire sauce bottle.) Fill with good dry sherry or olive oil and use as required, topping up as the sherry or oil is used. Add to dishes with caution as you may need only a very few drops.

HORSERADISH SAUCE

Makes about 300 ml/½ pint/1¼ cups

	Metric	Imperial	American
Grated horseradish	*225 g*	*8 oz*	*1 cup*
Caster (superfine) sugar	*1 tsp*	*1 tsp*	*1 tsp*
Prepared English mustard	*1 tsp*	*1 tsp*	*1 tsp*
Salt and pepper			
Plain yogurt	*250 ml*	*8 fl oz*	*1 cup*

1. Mix together the horseradish, sugar, mustard and seasoning. Stir in the yogurt.

2. Serve with beef and cold meats, or use in dips and sauces. This sauce is particularly good with beetroot.

SAUCE SOUBISE

Makes about 600 ml/1 pint/2½ cups

	Metric	Imperial	American
Butter or margarine	50 g	2 oz	¼ cup
Onions, finely chopped	6	6	6
Béchamel sauce (see page 14)	250 ml	8 fl oz	1 cup
Pinch of caster (superfine) sugar			
Salt if needed			
Plain yogurt	2 tbsp	2 tbsp	2 tbsp

1. Heat half the butter or margarine in a frying-pan (skillet) and sauté the onions for 10–15 minutes until brown. Stir in the Béchamel sauce, sugar and a little salt if necessary.

2. Continue to cook very gently for 30 minutes, then pass through a sieve. Cut the remaining butter or margarine in pieces and stir into the sauce with the yogurt. Stir well.

3. Serve with meat, poultry or vegetables.

YOGURT DRESSING

Makes about 250 ml/8 fl oz/1 cup

	Metric	Imperial	American
Plain yogurt	*250 ml*	*8 fl oz*	*1 cup*
Lemon juice			
Salt and pepper			

1. Beat the yogurt until smooth and stir in a little lemon juice.

2. Add salt and pepper to taste.

Variations
Garlic Dressing: Add ¼ tsp garlic salt or one freshly crushed garlic clove.
Honey Dressing: Add 1 tbsp honey and extra lemon juice to taste.
Russian Dressing: Add 1 tsp each of finely chopped gherkin, red pepper and chives, and ½ tsp celery seeds.
Herb Dressing: Add chopped fresh herbs, such as parsley, chives, chervil, basil, lemon balm, marjoram, oregano, etc.

HONEY DRESSING

Makes about 350 ml/12 fl oz/1½ cups

	Metric	Imperial	American
Clear honey	1 tbsp	1 tbsp	1 tbsp
Olive oil	250 ml	8 fl oz	1 cup
Wine vinegar	120 ml	4 fl oz	½ cup

1. Place all the ingredients in a blender or food processor and blend for 1 minute.

2. Alternatively, shake together in a screw-topped jar.

VINAIGRETTE

Makes about 150 ml/¼ pint/⅔ cup

	Metric	Imperial	American
Olive oil	6 tbsp	6 tbsp	6 tbsp
Tarragon vinegar	2 tbsp	2 tbsp	2 tbsp
Honey	2 tsp	2 tsp	2 tsp
Chopped capers	½ tsp	½ tsp	½ tsp
Chopped onion	½ tsp	½ tsp	½ tsp
Good pinch of basil, fennel or dill			
Chopped fresh mint	½ tsp	½ tsp	½ tsp

1. Combine all the ingredients thoroughly by shaking together in a screw-topped jar or beating together in a bowl.

2. Shake or stir again just before using.

YOGURT MAYONNAISE

Makes about 900 ml/1½ pints/3¾ cups

	Metric	Imperial	American
Cornflour (cornstarch)	1¼ tbsp	1¼ tbsp	1¼ tbsp
Salt	½ tsp	½ tsp	½ tsp
Mustard powder	½ tsp	½ tsp	½ tsp
Honey	1 tsp	1 tsp	1 tsp
Water	450 ml	¾ pint	2 cups
Vinegar	120 ml	4 fl oz	½ cup
Egg yolks	2	2	2
Olive oil	120 ml	4 fl oz	½ cup
Plain yogurt	120 ml	4 fl oz	½ cup

1. Place all the ingredients, except the egg yolks, oil and yogurt, in a saucepan. Cook very slowly, stirring continuously, until the mixture thickens. Boil for 1 minute, then remove from the heat and leave to cool a little.

2. Beat in the egg yolks, one at a time, and then beat in the oil very gradually. Chill in the refrigerator.

3. Stir in the yogurt 1 hour before serving.

HONEY MAYONNAISE

Makes about 450 ml/¾ pint/2 cups

	Metric	Imperial	American
Egg yolks	2	2	2
Clear honey	1–2 tbsp	1–2 tbsp	1–2 tbsp
Prepared mustard	1 tsp	1 tsp	1 tsp
Pinch of salt			
Pinch of cayenne pepper			
Olive oil	300 ml	½ pint	1¼ cups
Tarragon vinegar	1 tsp	1 tsp	1 tsp
Juice of 2 lemons			

1. Place the egg yolks in a bowl and add the honey, mustard, salt and cayenne pepper. Stir with a wooden spoon to mix.

2. Beat in the oil drop by drop, always beating the same way, until the mixture takes on the consistency of batter. If the mixture curdles, and will not improve with beating, beat another egg yolk in another bowl and gradually add it to the mayonnaise, beating all the time.

3. When the mayonnaise is quite stiff, stir in the vinegar and lemon juice.

CURRY DIP

Makes about 300 ml/½ pint/1¼ cups

	Metric	Imperial	American
Curry powder	*1 tsp*	*1 tsp*	*1 tsp*
Pinch of ground cumin			
Plain yogurt	*300 ml*	*½ pint*	*1¼ cups*
Cucumber, finely chopped	*½*	*½*	*½*

1. Blend the curry powder and the cumin with a small amount of the yogurt, then add the remainder, stirring well.

2. Add the chopped cucumber and serve with vegetable crudités or small crackers.

GARLIC DIP

Makes about 300 ml/½ pint/1¼ cups

	Metric	Imperial	American
Plain yogurt	300 ml	½ pint	1¼ cups
Garlic cloves, crushed or	2	2	2
garlic salt	1 tsp	1 tsp	1 tsp
Chopped chives	1 tsp	1 tsp	1 tsp
Salt and pepper			

1. Combine all the ingredients, stirring well.

2. Chill in the refrigerator before serving with vegetable crudités or small savoury crackers.

AVOCADO DIP

Serves 4

	Metric	Imperial	American
Avocados	2	2	2
Pinch of salt			
Lemon juice			
Yogurt cheese (see page 11)	225 g	8 oz	1 cup
Paprika			

1. Cut the avocados in half, remove the stones (seeds), scoop out the flesh and mash, adding the salt and lemon juice to taste.

2. Beat in the yogurt cheese and transfer to a serving bowl. Sprinkle liberally with paprika.

WALDORF DIP

Makes about 300 ml/½ pint/1¼ cups

	Metric	Imperial	American
Eating apples	*2*	*2*	*2*
Plain yogurt	*300 ml*	*½ pint*	*1¼ cups*
Stick of celery, chopped	*1*	*1*	*1*
Chopped walnuts	*1 tbsp*	*1 tbsp*	*1 tbsp*
Raisins	*50 g*	*2 oz*	*⅓ cup*
Pinch of salt			
Pinch of curry powder			
Pinch of paprika			

1. Core and dice the apples and add immediately to the yogurt.

2. Add the celery, walnuts and raisins. Season with the salt and curry powder and chill in the refrigerator.

3. Sprinkle with the paprika just before serving with potato crisps (chips) and small savoury crackers.

TOMATO DIP

Makes about 450 ml/¾ pint/2 cups

	Metric	Imperial	American
Plain yogurt	300 ml	½ pint	1¼ cups
Tomato ketchup	150 ml	¼ pint	⅔ cup
Pinch of garlic salt			
Dijon mustard	1 tsp	1 tsp	1 tsp
Salt and pepper			
Chopped fresh parsley	1 tbsp	1 tbsp	1 tbsp

1. Blend all the ingredients together well.

2. Chill in the refrigerator before serving with vegetable crudités or small savoury crackers.

PLUM AND CARROT DIP

Serves 4

	Metric	Imperial	American
Ripe plums, peeled and stoned (pitted)	450 g	1 lb	1 lb
Icing (confectioners') sugar	1 tsp	1 tsp	1 tsp
Plain yogurt	300 ml	½ pint	1¼ cups
Carrots, finely chopped	450 g	1 lb	1 lb

1. Mash the plums with the sugar and beat into the yogurt.

2. Stir in the chopped carrots, transfer to a serving bowl and serve as a dip with fresh vegetable crudités.

Variation
If the carrots are small, young ones, do not chop and add to the dip but cut into sticks and use for dipping instead.

LIPTAUER CHEESE

Makes about 300 g/10 oz/1¼ cups

	Metric	Imperial	American
Butter or margarine	*100 g*	*4 oz*	*½ cup*
Yogurt cheese (see page 11)	*100 g*	*4 oz*	*½ cup*
Anchovy essence	*3 tsp*	*3 tsp*	*3 tsp*
Chopped capers	*2 tsp*	*2 tsp*	*2 tsp*
Chopped gherkins	*2 tsp*	*2 tsp*	*2 tsp*
Caraway seeds	*1 tsp*	*1 tsp*	*1 tsp*
Paprika	*1 tsp*	*1 tsp*	*1 tsp*
Dijon mustard	*1 tsp*	*1 tsp*	*1 tsp*
Pinch of celery salt			

1. Cream the butter or margarine and gradually add the other ingredients, beating well until the texture is light.

2. This cheese will keep for two weeks if stored, covered, in the refrigerator. Serve with crudités.

WHITE RUSSIAN

Makes about 300 g/10 oz/1¼ cups

	Metric	Imperial	American
Yogurt cheese (see page 11)	*225 g*	*8 oz*	*1 cup*
Finely minced (ground) onion	*1 tsp*	*1 tsp*	*1 tsp*
Small jar of mock caviar			
Lemon wedges to serve			

1. Combine the cheese with the minced onion, then carefully fold in the mock caviar.

2. Top with lemon wedges before serving.

2
STARTERS AND SOUPS

EGGS FLORENTINE

Serves 4

	Metric	Imperial	American
Frozen spinach, thawed	*350 g*	*12 oz*	*1½ cups*
Plain yogurt	*150 ml*	*¼ pint*	*⅔ cup*
Pinch of ground nutmeg			
Salt and pepper			
Eggs	*4*	*4*	*4*

1. Drain the spinach well and mix with the yogurt and nutmeg. Season to taste with salt and pepper.

2. Spoon the mixture into four ramekins (custard cups), building it up at the sides to make 'nests'. Break an egg into each 'nest'.

3. Bake in the oven at 375°F/190°C (Gas Mark 5) for 10–15 minutes until the eggs have set.

WALDORF SLAW

Serves 4

	Metric	Imperial	American
White cabbage	225 g	8 oz	1/2 lb
Small can of mandarins, drained			
Raisins	50 g	2 oz	1/3 cup
Walnuts, chopped	50 g	2 oz	1/2 cup
Stick of celery, chopped			
Ground ginger	1/4 tsp	1/4 tsp	1/4 tsp
Yogurt mayonnaise (see page 21)	300 ml	1/2 pint	1 1/4 cups
Salt and pepper if needed			
Eating apples	2	2	2

Garnish
Black grapes
Tomato slices
Lettuce leaves

1. Shred the cabbage and place in a bowl with the mandarin segments, raisins, walnuts and celery.

2. Add the ground ginger to the mayonnaise, season if necessary with salt and pepper, and mix into the cabbage until all the ingredients are well coated.

3. Core and finely slice the apples and mix lightly into the slaw.

4. For the garnish, halve and pip (seed) the grapes. Serve the slaw in individual dishes, garnished with grapes, tomato slices and lettuce leaves.

KIPPER COLE SLAW

Serves 2–3

	Metric	Imperial	American
Fresh kipper (kippered herring) fillets	*225 g*	*8 oz*	*½ lb*
White wine	*120 ml*	*4 fl oz*	*½ cup*
Olive oil	*2 tbsp*	*2 tbsp*	*2 tbsp*
Plain yogurt	*175 ml*	*6 fl oz*	*¾ cup*
Clear honey	*1 tsp*	*1 tsp*	*1 tsp*
Lemon juice	*1 tbsp*	*1 tbsp*	*1 tbsp*
Pinch of black pepper			
Small white cabbage, finely shredded	*½*	*½*	*½*

Garnish
Tomato slices
Lettuce

1. Marinate the kipper fillets overnight in the wine and oil.

2. Mix the yogurt, honey, lemon juice and pepper together. Add the cabbage and toss well.

3. Drain and skin the kipper fillets. Roll the fillets, cut in strips and arrange on top of the cabbage mixture.

4. Garnish with tomato slices and lettuce.

COUPE CAPRICE

Serves 6

	Metric	Imperial	American
Small Charantais melon	*1*	*1*	*1*
Shrimps, peeled	*175 g*	*6 oz*	*1 cup*
Green pepper, cored, seeded and finely diced	*1*	*1*	*1*
Lemon juice	*1 tsp*	*1 tsp*	*1 tsp*
Pinch of salt			
Plain yogurt or Yogurt mayonnaise (see page 21)	*300 ml*	*1/2 pint*	*1 1/4 cups*
Pinch of paprika			

1. Cut the melon in slices and remove the seeds. Peel and dice the flesh finely.

2. Mix the shrimps, melon and pepper together and sprinkle with lemon juice and salt. Add the yogurt or mayonnaise and fold in carefully.

3. Serve in coupe or cocktail glasses, sprinkled with paprika and well chilled. A few shrimps and green pepper strips can be retained for garnish.

LEMON CRAB

Serves 4

	Metric	Imperial	American
Punnet of cress	*1*	*1*	*1*
Small can of crabmeat, drained			
Hard-boiled (hard-cooked) eggs, chopped	*3*	*3*	*3*
Pinch of black pepper			
Lemon juice	*1 tsp*	*1 tsp*	*1 tsp*
Finely grated lemon rind	*1 tsp*	*1 tsp*	*1 tsp*
Yogurt mayonnaise (see page 21)	*150 ml*	*¼ pint*	*⅔ cup*

1. Cut, wash and drain the cress. Sprinkle a little cress in the bottom of four sundae glasses.

2. Coarsely chop the crabmeat and mix lightly with the chopped egg. Season with pepper.

3. Add the lemon juice and grated lemon rind to the mayonnaise, then add to the egg and crabmeat, mixing well.

4. Pile the mixture into the glasses and sprinkle the remaining cress round the edge.

DEVILLED HAM PÂTÉ

Serves 4

	Metric	Imperial	American
Butter or margarine	*50 g*	*2 oz*	*¼ cup*
Yogurt cheese (see page 11)	*50 g*	*2 oz*	*¼ cup*
Salt and pepper			
Few drops of chilli sauce (see page 16)			
Ham, chopped	*50 g*	*2 oz*	*½ cup*
To serve			
Toast triangles			
Lettuce leaves			
Tomato slices			
Cucumber slices			

1. Cream the butter or margarine with the yogurt cheese. Season with salt, pepper and chilli sauce, then fold in the ham.

2. Spread liberally on toast triangles and serve on lettuce leaves with slices of tomato and cucumber.

SHERRIED GRAPEFRUIT

Serves 4

	Metric	Imperial	American
Grapefruit	2	2	2
Sweet sherry	4 tbsp	4 tbsp	4 tbsp
Clear honey	4 tsp	4 tsp	4 tsp
Butter	25 g	1 oz	2 tbsp

1. Halve the grapefruit, cut out the centre cores and loosen the segments with a sharp knife or grapefruit knife.

2. Pour 1 tbsp sherry and 1 tsp honey into the centre of each grapefruit half and add a knob of butter.

3. Arrange the grapefruit halves in a shallow ovenproof dish and bake at 400°F/200°C (Gas Mark 6) for about 15 minutes. Pour over any juice that has run out of the fruit and serve hot.

PRAWN VOL-AU-VENTS

Serves 4

	Metric	Imperial	American
Butter	*40 g*	*1½ oz*	*3 tbsp*
Mushrooms, sliced	*225 g*	*8 oz*	*2 cups*
Peeled prawns (shrimp)	*225 g*	*8 oz*	*1½ cups*
Plain yogurt	*150 ml*	*¼ pint*	*⅔ cup*
Salt and pepper			
7.5 cm/3 inch vol-au-vent cases, baked	*4*	*4*	*4*
Lettuce leaves or cress to garnish			

1. Melt the butter in a frying-pan (skillet) and sauté the mushrooms for about 3 minutes. Add the prawns and cook gently for a further 3 minutes. Stir in the yogurt and season to taste with salt and pepper.

2. Place the vol-au-vent cases on a baking sheet and fill with the prawn mixture. Bake in the oven at 400°F/200°C (Gas Mark 6) for 10 minutes.

3. Serve hot or cold, garnished with lettuce or cress.

AZTEC

Serves 1–2

	Metric	Imperial	American
Small green pepper, cored, *seeded and chopped*	*1*	*1*	*1*
Butter	*1 tsp*	*1 tsp*	*1 tsp*
Egg, beaten	*1*	*1*	*1*
Salt and pepper			
Yogurt cheese (see page 11)	*100 g*	*4 oz*	*½ cup*

1. Cook the green pepper in the butter for 3 minutes. Add the egg and season with salt and pepper. Heat gently and, as the mixture begins to set, add the yogurt cheese. Continue to cook for about 1 minute, stirring.

2. Serve with a green salad or on toast.

BORSCHT

Serves 4–6

	Metric	Imperial	American
Butter or margarine	50 g	2 oz	¼ cup
Medium onion, chopped	1	1	1
Raw beetroot (beet), coarsely grated	225 g	8 oz	½ lb
Tomatoes, chopped	2	2	2
Potato, grated	1	1	1
Garlic clove, crushed	1	1	1
Beef stock	1.2 litres	2 pints	5 cups
Cabbage, grated	225 g	8 oz	½ lb
Vinegar	2 tbsp	2 tbsp	2 tbsp
Salt and pepper			
Plain yogurt	4–6 tbsp	4–6 tbsp	4–6 tbsp
Chopped fresh parsley or dill to serve			

1. Heat the butter or margarine in a saucepan and cook the onion for 5 minutes. Add the beetroot (beet), tomato, potato, garlic and half the stock. Cook for 15 minutes.

2. Add the remaining stock, the cabbage and vinegar. Season to taste with salt and pepper and cook for a further 30 minutes.

3. Serve in individual soup plates with a spoonful of yogurt and a sprinkling of chopped parsley or dill.

JAJIK

This is considered the classic cold yogurt soup and is found in many parts of the world where yogurt constitutes a large part of the staple diet.

Serves 4

	Metric	Imperial	American
Medium cucumber	1	1	1
Salt and pepper			
Garlic clove, crushed	1	1	1
Chopped fresh mint leaves	1 tsp	1 tsp	1 tsp
Chopped fresh or dried fennel	½ tsp	½ tsp	½ tsp
Wine vinegar	1 tsp	1 tsp	1 tsp
Olive oil	1 tsp	1 tsp	1 tsp
Plain yogurt	450 ml	¾ pint	2 cups
Cold water	300 ml	½ pint	1¼ cups
Ice cubes to serve			
Chopped fresh mint to garnish			

1. Peel the cucumber, halve lengthways and scoop out the seeds. Chop the flesh finely and sprinkle with salt. Leave for about 1 hour, then rinse and drain well.

2. Combine the garlic, herbs, vinegar, oil and yogurt. Add the water to make a thin cream and fold in the cucumber. Season with salt and pepper.

3. Chill for at least 2 hours before serving in chilled soup plates. Add a few ice cubes to each plate and sprinkle with chopped mint.

WATERCRESS SOUP

Serves 4

	Metric	Imperial	American
Butter or margarine	100 g	4 oz	1/2 cup
Plain (all-purpose) flour	50 g	2 oz	1/2 cup
Chicken stock	600 ml	1 pint	2 1/2 cups
Milk or single (light) cream	150 ml	1/4 pint	2/3 cup
Salt and pepper			
Finely chopped onion	50 g	2 oz	1/2 cup
Bunches of watercress	3	3	3
Plain yogurt	4 tbsp	4 tbsp	4 tbsp
Chopped watercress to garnish			

1. Make a roux by melting 75 g/3 oz/6 tbsp butter or margarine in a heavy saucepan and stirring in the flour. Cook for 1–2 minutes without colouring.

2. Remove the pan from the heat and gradually stir in the stock and milk or cream. Bring to the boil, stirring continuously. Simmer for 3 minutes, stirring, and season with salt and pepper.

3. Cook the onion in the remaining butter or margarine for about 5 minutes until soft but not coloured.

4. Wash the watercress thoroughly and chop coarsely, using about half the stems. Add to the onions, place the lid on the pan and cook very slowly for about 5 minutes.

5. Add the onion and watercress to the sauce and place in a blender or food processor. Blend until smooth. Alternatively, pass the soup through a sieve.

6. Reheat the soup, taste and adjust the seasoning. Serve, adding a spoonful of yogurt to each plate. Garnish with chopped watercress.

CHICKEN AVOCADO SOUP

Serves 2–3

	Metric	Imperial	American
Ripe avocado	1	1	1
Chicken stock, chilled	300 ml	½ pint	1¼ cups
Chopped chives	1 tsp	1 tsp	1 tsp
Few drops of chilli sauce (see page 16)			
Salt and pepper			
Plain yogurt	4 tbsp	4 tbsp	4 tbsp

1. Peel and stone (seed) the avocado. Coarsely chop the avocado flesh and place in a blender or food processor with the chilled stock and chives.

2. Blend for about 20 seconds, then press the mixture through a fairly fine sieve into a bowl.

3. Add the chilli sauce and season with salt and pepper. Stir in the yogurt. Chill for at least 1 hour before serving with crusty bread.

APPLE AND WINE SOUP

Serves 4

	Metric	Imperial	American
Sugar	75 g	3 oz	6 tbsp
Pinch of salt			
Cooking (tart) apples, peeled, cored and diced	1.5 kg	3 lb	3 lb
Dry white breadcrumbs	6 tbsp	6 tbsp	6 tbsp
Cinnamon stick	1	1	1
Thinly pared rind of 1 lemon			
Dry red wine	450 ml	¾ pint	2 cups
Juice of 2 lemons			
Redcurrant jelly	3 tbsp	3 tbsp	3 tbsp
Plain yogurt	4 tbsp	4 tbsp	4 tbsp

1. Put the sugar and salt in a saucepan, add 600 ml/1 pint/2½ cups water and bring to the boil. Add the apples, breadcrumbs, cinnamon and lemon rind, and cook, stirring, for 5–10 minutes, until the apples are soft. Remove the cinnamon and lemon rind.

2. Pour the apple mixture into a blender or food processor and blend until smooth. Alternatively, press through a sieve.

3. Return the mixture to the pan and add the wine, lemon juice and redcurrant jelly. Simmer gently, stirring continuously, until the jelly dissolves and the soup is warmed through.

4. Transfer the soup to four individual serving bowls and top each one with 1 tbsp yogurt.

ORANGE AND CARROT SOUP

Serves 4

	Metric	Imperial	American
Baby carrots	450 g	1 lb	1 lb
Chicken stock	450 ml	¾ pint	2 cups
Can of frozen concentrated orange juice			
Salt and pepper			
Plain yogurt	4 tbsp	4 tbsp	4 tbsp

1. Cook the carrots in boiling salted water for about 10 minutes until tender. Drain and blend to a purée in a blender or food processor.

2. Add the stock to the carrot purée and bring to the boil. Add the orange juice and heat gently until thawed. Simmer for 5 minutes and season to taste with salt and pepper.

3. Serve in warmed soup plates with 1 tbsp yogurt added to each.

CURRY AND APPLE SOUP

Serves 6

	Metric	Imperial	American
Butter	25 g	1 oz	2 tbsp
Onion, chopped	1	1	1
Plain (all-purpose) flour	40 g	1½ oz	6 tbsp
Curry powder	1 tbsp	1 tbsp	1 tbsp
Chicken stock	900 ml	1½ pints	3¾ cups
Cooking (tart) apples, peeled, cored and thinly sliced	750 g	1½ lb	1½ lb
Squeeze of lemon juice			
Salt and pepper			
Plain yogurt	6 tbsp	6 tbsp	6 tbsp

1. Heat the butter in a frying-pan (skillet) and sauté the onion for 5 minutes until soft.

2. Stir in the flour and curry powder and cook for 1 minute, stirring. Add the stock, apples and lemon juice and bring to the boil, stirring continuously. Season to taste with salt and pepper.

3. Serve in warmed soup plates with 1 tbsp yogurt added to each.

CURRY AND RICE SOUP

Serves 6

	Metric	Imperial	American
Butter	25 g	1 oz	2 tbsp
Onion, chopped	1	1	1
Curry powder	1 tbsp	1 tbsp	1 tbsp
Plain (all-purpose) flour	1 tbsp	1 tbsp	1 tbsp
Beef or chicken stock	900 ml	1½ pints	5 cups
Celery sticks, sliced	2	2	2
Long-grain rice	50 g	2 oz	½ cup
Plain yogurt	6 tbsp	6 tbsp	6 tbsp

1. Heat the butter in a frying-pan (skillet) and sauté the onion for 5 minutes until soft.

2. Add the curry powder and cook for 2 minutes. Stir in the flour and add the stock.

3. Bring to the boil and add the celery and rice. Simmer for about 15 minutes until the rice is tender.

4. Serve in warmed soup plates with 1 tbsp yogurt added to each.

3
MAIN MEALS

LAMB CHOP SKILLET

Serves 4

	Metric	Imperial	American
Butter or oil for frying			
Lamb chops	*4*	*4*	*4*
Tomatoes	*4*	*4*	*4*
Dry white wine	*120 ml*	*4 fl oz*	*½ cup*
Plain yogurt	*120 ml*	*4 fl oz*	*½ cup*
Salt and pepper			
Chopped fresh basil			

1. Heat a little butter or oil in a frying-pan (skillet), add the chops and cook until brown on both sides.

2. Add the tomatoes, whole or cut into quarters, and cook very slowly, covered, until the chops are almost tender.

3. Add the wine and yogurt and season to taste with salt, pepper and basil. Simmer gently for another 10 minutes before serving.

LAMB KEBABS

Serves 4

	Metric	Imperial	American
Boned leg of lamb, cut in 2.5–cm/1–inch cubes	900 g	2 lb	2 lb
Small firm tomatoes, halved	4	4	4
Green pepper, cored, seeded and cut in 2.5–cm/1–inch sections	1	1	1
Small aubergines (eggplants), thinly sliced	2	2	2
Bay leaves	16	16	16
Salt and pepper			
Marinade			
Olive oil	1 tbsp	1 tbsp	1 tbsp
Juice of ½ lemon			
Plain yogurt	1 tbsp	1 tbsp	1 tbsp

1. To prepare the marinade, mix all the ingredients together. Pour over the lamb and leave to marinate for at least 5 hours, turning occasionally.

2. Thread the meat and vegetables onto eight kebab skewers, adding two bay leaves to each one. Season to taste with salt and pepper.

3. Heat the grill (broiler) to high and cook the kebabs, turning frequently, for 10–15 minutes until the meat is tender. Serve on a bed of boiled brown rice.

Variations
Add mushrooms or kidneys to the kebabs and add various herbs to the marinade.

HONEY GLAZED BACON

Serves 6

	Metric	Imperial	American
1.5–1.8 kg/3–4 lb boned and rolled forehock of bacon	*1*	*1*	*1*
Bay leaf	*1*	*1*	*1*
Blade of mace	*1*	*1*	*1*
A few peppercorns			
A few cloves			
Clear honey	*3 tbsp*	*3 tbsp*	*3 tbsp*
Juice of 1 orange			
Cornflour (cornstarch)	*1 tbsp*	*1 tbsp*	*1 tbsp*
Salt and pepper			

1. Place the bacon in a large saucepan with the bay leaf, mace, peppercorns and cloves. Cover with water, bring to the boil and simmer for 50 minutes. Drain, reserving 300 ml/½ pint/1¼ cups stock for gravy.

2. Place the bacon joint in a roasting tin (pan) and score the rind by cutting in a diamond pattern. Mix together the honey and orange juice and slowly pour over the bacon so that the glaze soaks into the incisions in the rind.

3. Roast in the oven at 350°F/180°C (Gas Mark 4) for 50–60 minutes until tender. Remove the bacon to a heated serving plate, remove the string and pour over the pan drippings.

4. To make the gravy, blend the cornflour with a little of the cold reserved stock, then stir back into the

remaining stock. Bring to the boil, stirring, and cook until thickened. Season to taste with salt and pepper.

Note
Season the gravy cautiously as the stock will be salty.

BOEUF STROGANOFF

Serves 4–6

	Metric	Imperial	American
Lean steak	900 g	2 lb	2 lb
Plain (all-purpose) flour	1 tbsp	1 tbsp	1 tbsp
Vegetable oil	2 tbsp	2 tbsp	2 tbsp
Medium onion, sliced	1	1	1
Tomato purée (paste)	2 tbsp	2 tbsp	2 tbsp
Salt and pepper			
Button mushrooms, thinly sliced	225 g	8 oz	2 cups
Brandy	1 tbsp	1 tbsp	1 tbsp
Plain yogurt	300 ml	½ pint	1¼ cups

1. Cut the steak into very small strips and dredge with flour.

2. Heat the oil in a heavy frying-pan (skillet) and cook the onion for 5 minutes until soft but not coloured. Add the meat, tomato purée and seasoning and cook for 5 minutes more.

3. Add the mushrooms and cook for a further few minutes. Stir in the brandy and yogurt and heat again slowly.

OSLO CHOPS

Serves 4

	Metric	Imperial	American
Neck (rib) of lamb chops	*8*	*8*	*8*
Seasoned flour			
Oil for frying			
Chicken stock	*250 ml*	*8 fl oz*	*1 cup*
Wine vinegar	*1½ tbsp*	*1½ tbsp*	*1½ tbsp*
Tomato purée (paste)	*1½ tbsp*	*1½ tbsp*	*1½ tbsp*
Plain yogurt	*1½ tbsp*	*1½ tbsp*	*1½ tbsp*
Honey	*2 tsp*	*2 tsp*	*2 tsp*
Worcestershire sauce	*1 tsp*	*1 tsp*	*1 tsp*
Yeast extract	*2 tsp*	*2 tsp*	*2 tsp*
Onions, sliced	*2*	*2*	*2*
Salt and pepper			

1. Coat the chops with seasoned flour.

2. Heat a little oil in a frying-pan (skillet) and fry the chops until brown. Place in an ovenproof dish.

3. Mix together all the other ingredients, except the onions, salt and pepper, and pour over the chops. Top with the sliced onions and season to taste with salt and pepper.

4. Cover and bake in the oven at 400°F/200°C (Gas Mark 6) until boiling, then reduce the oven temperature to 300°F/150°C (Gas Mark 2) and cook for 1½–2 hours until the chops are tender.

Variation
Try spare-ribs cooked this way.

BARBECUE PORK CHOPS

Serves 4

	Metric	Imperial	American
Pork chops	4	4	4
Barbecue sauce (see page 16)	120 ml	4 fl oz	½ cup

1. Place the chops on the grill (broiler) grid and brush with barbecue sauce. Cook under a hot grill for about 5 minutes, then turn the chops and brush again.

2. Continue cooking the chops, turning and brushing frequently, for 20–30 minutes, until well done.

Variation
Try pork sausages cooked this way.

INDIAN PILAU

This is a traditional dish, well worth the trouble of preparation. Mangoes are available but can be expensive: One will suffice. Do not, in the interest of economy, substitute mango chutney!

Serves 6–8

	Metric	Imperial	American
Long-grain rice	900 g	2 lb	2 lb
Garlic cloves	2	2	2
Fresh root ginger, peeled	25 g	1 oz	1½ tbsp
Coriander	1 tsp	1 tsp	1 tsp
White peppercorns	4	4	4
Cloves	5	5	5
Cardamom pods	5	5	5
Margarine	50 g	2 oz	¼ cup
Onions, sliced	2	2	2
Lean mutton or lamb, diced	900 g	2 lb	2 lb
Plain yogurt	600 ml	1 pint	2½ cups
Salt			
Pinch of saffron threads			
Pistachios, slivered (shredded)	100 g	4 oz	1 cup
Grapes, peeled, halved and seeded	50 g	2 oz	½ cup
Chopped ripe mango	100 g	4 oz	1 cup
Orange, peeled and segmented	1	1	1

1. Wash the rice well and soak in cold water for 30 minutes.

2. Meanwhile, pound the garlic, ginger, coriander, peppercorns, cloves and cardamom pods and mix well together.

3. Place the margarine, onions and mutton or lamb in a pan, add the yogurt and pounded spice mixture and heat slightly. Add salt to taste and mix well. Drain the uncooked rice and place on top of the lamb mixture.

4. Soak the saffron in a little water and pour it over the centre of the rice, sprinkling the nuts, grapes, mango and orange on top.

5. Cook over a high heat for 10 minutes, making sure it does not burn, then cook very slowly for about 20 minutes until the meat and rice are tender.

MOUSSAKA

Serves 6

	Metric	Imperial	American
Medium aubergines (eggplants)	2	2	2
Salt and pepper			
Oil for frying			
Onions, chopped	2	2	2
Garlic clove, crushed	1	1	1
Lean shoulder lamb, minced (ground)	700 g	1½ lb	1½ lb
Plain (all-purpose) flour	1 tbsp	1 tbsp	1 tbsp
Medium can of tomato juice			
Mixed dried herbs	½ tsp	½ tsp	½ tsp
Topping			
Egg	1	1	1
Plain yogurt	150 ml	¼ pint	⅔ cup
Salt and pepper			

1. Slice the aubergines thinly, sprinkle liberally with salt and leave for 30 minutes, then rinse and drain.

2. Fry the aubergine slices in the minimum of oil until golden brown on both sides. Drain on kitchen paper towels.

3. Fry the onions, garlic and minced lamb in 1 tbsp oil for about 10 minutes, blend in the flour, add the tomato juice and herbs and season to taste with salt and pepper. Bring to the boil, stirring continuously.

4. Layer the aubergine slices and meat mixture in an ovenproof dish, finishing with a layer of aubergine.

Pour over enough liquid from the meat mixture to moisten.

5. For the topping, beat the egg and mix in the yogurt and seasoning. Pour over the moussaka.

6. Bake in the oven at 375°F/190°C (Gas Mark 5) for about 45 minutes, or until the topping is set.

Variation
Substitute sliced potato and tomato for aubergine and increase the herb flavouring.

TURKISH LAMB WITH RICE

Serves 6—8

	Metric	Imperial	American
Boned shoulder of lamb	1	1	1
Butter or margarine	50 g	2 oz	1/4 cup
Clear honey	1 tbsp	1 tbsp	1 tbsp
Long-grain rice	450 g	1 lb	3 cups
Few cardamom pods			
Cinnamon stick	1	1	1
Marinade			
Garlic cloves	2	2	2
Small piece of fresh root ginger, peeled			
Few drops of chilli sauce (see page 16)			
Plain yogurt	150 ml	1/4 pint	2/3 cup
Juice of 1 lemon			
Salt and pepper			
Stuffing			
Lamb kidneys, skinned and cored	2	2	2
Blanched almonds	25 g	1 oz	1/4 cup
Raisins	100 g	4 oz	2/3 cup
Pistachio nuts, chopped	50 g	2 oz	1/2 cup
Salt and pepper			
Plain yogurt	150 ml	1/4 pint	2/3 cup

1. Slash the flesh of the lamb to allow the marinade to penetrate.

2. To make the marinade, pound the garlic and ginger

together, then add the chilli sauce, yogurt and lemon juice. Season to taste with salt and pepper and mix to a paste. (Alternatively, blend all the ingredients together in a blender or food processor.)

3. Spread the paste over the lamb, inside and out, and leave overnight.

4. The next day, make the stuffing. Place the lamb kidneys in a saucepan with a little water and simmer for about 20 minutes until tender. Drain, reserving the cooking liquid, and chop.

5. Reserve a few whole almonds and some raisins to add to the rice. Chop the remaining almonds.

6. Mix the chopped pistachios and almonds, remaining raisins and kidney cooking liquid with the chopped kidneys. Season with salt and pepper and add enough yogurt to make a stiff paste. Use to stuff the inside of the lamb shoulder, pressing the stuffing in tightly.

7. Roll up the lamb and secure with skewers and string. Place in a large, deep ovenproof casserole with half the butter or margarine. Cover and cook in the oven at 350°F/180°C (Gas Mark 4) for 1 hour.

8. Turn the meat and pour over the honey. Cook for a further 2 hours or until tender, basting frequently with the juices.

9. Cook the rice in boiling salted water until tender. Meanwhile, heat the remaining butter or margarine in a pan with the cardamom and cinnamon and fry the reserved whole almonds and raisins until the almonds are browned.

10. When the rice is cooked, drain well and stir in the almonds and raisins, discarding the spices.

11. Place the stuffed shoulder of lamb on a heated serving dish and remove skewers and string. Surround with the rice mixture. Skim the lamb cooking juice to remove the fat and serve separately, thickened with arrowroot, if liked.

HONEY DUCK

Serves 6

	Metric	Imperial	American
2.3–2.6 kg/5–6 lb ovenready duck	*1*	*1*	*1*
Clear honey	*1 tbsp*	*1 tbsp*	*1 tbsp*
Juice of 1 orange			
Orange slices and watercress to garnish			
Stuffing			
Pork sausagemeat	*450 g*	*1 lb*	*1 lb*
Fresh breadcrumbs	*50 g*	*2 oz*	*1 cup*
Grated rind of 1 orange			
Dried mixed herbs	*½ tsp*	*½ tsp*	*½ tsp*
Salt and pepper			
Gravy			
Duck giblets			
Plain (all-purpose) flour	*1 tbsp*	*1 tbsp*	*1 tbsp*
Salt and pepper			

1. To make the stuffing, mix together all the ingredients, adding salt and pepper to taste. Pack into the duck and sew or skewer down the loose skin.

2. Place the duck on a rack in a roasting tin (pan) and prick the skin all over with a large needle. Rub the skin with salt and roast at 400°F/200°C (Gas Mark 6) for 30 minutes, then reduce the oven temperature to 350°F/180°C (Gas Mark 4) and continue cooking for another 1½ hours until nearly cooked.

3. Meanwhile, place the giblets in a saucepan, cover with 300 ml/½ pint/1¼ cups water, bring to the boil and simmer for 45 minutes-1 hour, then drain and reserve the stock for making gravy.

4. Mix together the honey and orange juice and brush all over the duck to glaze. Return to the oven and cook for a further 15 minutes.

5. When the duck is cooked, remove it from the roasting tin and keep warm. Pour most of the fat out of the tin, leaving about 2 tbsp. Add the flour, blend well and cook until beginning to brown. Remove from the heat and gradually stir in the stock. Boil for 2–3 minutes, stirring, until smooth and thick. Season well with salt and pepper.

6. Place the duck on a heated serving plate and garnish with watercress and orange slices. Serve the gravy separately.

TURKEY SUPREME

Serves 4–6

	Metric	Imperial	American
Curry powder	½ tsp	½ tsp	½ tsp
Tomato purée (paste)	1 tbsp	1 tbsp	1 tbsp
Lemon juice	1 tbsp	1 tbsp	1 tbsp
Apricot jam	1 tbsp	1 tbsp	1 tbsp
Small onion, very finely chopped	1	1	1
Garlic clove, crushed	1	1	1
Cooked turkey	450 g	1 lb	1 lb
Salt and pepper			
Yogurt mayonnaise (see page 21) or ½ plain yogurt, ½ mayonnaise	300 ml	½ pint	1¼ cups

Garnish
Chopped fresh parsley
Paprika

1. Place the curry powder, tomato purée (paste), lemon juice and jam in a pan and heat gently, bringing the mixture slowly to the boil, stirring continuously.

2. Add the onion and garlic and place in a blender or food processor. Blend to a smooth purée.

3. Chop the turkey fairly finely, season with salt and pepper and add to the purée. Fold in the mayonnaise and season again.

4. Chill overnight in the refrigerator and garnish with parsley and paprika just before serving with a green or rice salad.

TANDOORI CHICKEN

Serves 4

	Metric	Imperial	American
Chicken portions	*4*	*4*	*4*
Marinade			
Small piece of fresh root *ginger, peeled*			
Garlic cloves	*2*	*2*	*2*
Curry powder	*2 tsp*	*2 tsp*	*2 tsp*
Ground cumin	*¼ tsp*	*¼ tsp*	*¼ tsp*
Plain yogurt	*300 ml*	*½ pint*	*1¼ cups*
Few drops of chilli sauce *(see page 16)*			
Black pepper			

1. Prepare the marinade by putting all the ingredients in a blender or food processor and blending until smooth. Alternatively, pound the ginger, garlic, curry powder and cumin to a smooth paste, adding the yogurt, chilli sauce and pepper.
2. Skin the chicken portions and make a few cuts in the flesh of each one with a sharp knife.
3. Rub the chicken portions with the marinade and leave for at least 3 hours, turning occasionally.
4. Heat the grill (broiler) to high. Shake the chicken portions but do not wipe them. Cook under the grill until brown, turning once.
5. Reduce the heat to low and continue cooking for about 35 minutes until the chicken is tender.

CHICKEN GERMAN STYLE

Serves 4

	Metric	Imperial	American
Egg yolks	2	2	2
Cold water	2 tbsp	2 tbsp	2 tbsp
Chicken portions	4	4	4
Dry breadcrumbs	50 g	2 oz	½ cup
Parmesan cheese, grated	50 g	2 oz	½ cup
Butter or margarine	100 g	4 oz	½ cup
Mushrooms, sliced	175 g	6 oz	2 cups
Béchamel sauce (see page 14)	300 ml	½ pint	1¼ cups
Juice of ½ lemon			
Salt and pepper			
Glass of dry white wine			

1. Beat the egg yolks and dilute with the water. Dip the chicken portions in the egg and then coat with a mixture of the breadcrumbs and grated Parmesan.

2. Melt the butter or margarine in a frying-pan (skillet) and when hot lay the chicken portions in the pan. Cook until brown on all sides.

3. Lower the heat and cook, covered, until almost tender. (Alternatively, bake the chicken portions in the oven at 400°F/200°C/Gas Mark 6.)

4. Add the mushrooms to the chicken and cook for a few minutes more.

5. Stir the Béchamel sauce and lemon juice into the pan,

season to taste with salt and pepper and simmer for 10 minutes. Add the white wine just before serving.

CHICKEN CELESTE

Serves 4

	Metric	Imperial	American
Chicken portions	4	4	4
Salt and pepper			
Few streaky (fat) bacon rashers (slices)			
Clear honey	2 tbsp	2 tbsp	2 tbsp
Dijon mustard	1 tbsp	1 tbsp	1 tbsp
Curry powder	1 tsp	1 tsp	1 tsp
Garlic clove, crushed	1	1	1

1. Skin the chicken portions and lay them in an ovenproof dish. Sprinkle with salt and pepper and cover with the bacon rashers.

2. Mix together the remaining ingredients and pour over the chicken. Bake in the oven at 375°F/190°C (Gas Mark 5) for about 1 hour until the chicken portions are tender, turning them over half way through cooking and basting occasionally.

3. Serve with plain gravy *and* a sauce made from the pan drippings, if liked.

CHICKEN AND POTATO PIE

This dish is excellent for using up leftover chicken. The other ingredients can be reduced accordingly.

Serves 6

	Metric	Imperial	American
1.5 kg/3 lb chicken, cooked	1	1	1
Large potatoes, cooked	6	6	6
Butter	25 g	1 oz	2 tbsp
Egg, beaten	1	1	1
Plain yogurt	50 ml	2 fl oz	1/4 cup
Salt and pepper			
Bacon rashers (slices), derinded and diced	6	6	6
Cheddar cheese, grated	75 g	3 oz	3/4 cup

1. Skin the chicken, remove the meat from the bones and cut into small pieces.

2. Mash the potatoes and beat in the butter, egg and yogurt. Season to taste with salt and pepper.

3. Lightly fry the bacon in its own fat and drain on kitchen paper towels.

4. Place a layer of mashed potato in the bottom of an ovenproof dish and cover with a layer of chicken. Add another layer of potato, then a layer of bacon. Continue alternating layers, ending with a layer of mashed potato. Sprinkle the top of the pie with grated Cheddar cheese.

5. Bake in the oven at 375°F/190°C (Gas Mark 5) for about 45 minutes until the cheese is bubbling.

CHICKEN MOULD

Serves 4

	Metric	Imperial	American
Powdered (unflavored) gelatine	1 tbsp	1 tbsp	1 tbsp
Boiling chicken stock	175 ml	6 fl oz	¾ cup
Yogurt mayonnaise (see page 21)	175 ml	6 fl oz	¾ cup
Cold cooked chicken, diced	350 g	12 oz	3 cups
Salt and pepper			

1. Put 3 tbsp cold water in a small bowl and sprinkle over the gelatine. Leave for about 5 minutes to soften.

2. Pour the boiling chicken stock into a large bowl and stir in the gelatine. As it begins to set, beat it until it is frothy, then fold in the mayonnaise and diced chicken. Season to taste with salt and pepper, then transfer to a mould or soufflé dish and chill in the refrigerator until set.

3. Serve with a green salad.

STUFFED MARROW

Serves 4

	Metric	Imperial	American
Large marrow (squash)	1	1	1
Cooked rice	225 g	8 oz	1½ cups
Cooked chicken, chopped	225 g	8 oz	½ lb
Bay leaf	1	1	1
Cardamom pods, cracked	2	2	2
Cloves	2	2	2
Plain yogurt	250 ml	8 fl oz	1 cup
Butter	1 tbsp	1 tbsp	1 tbsp
Plain (all-purpose) flour	2 tbsp	2 tbsp	2 tbsp
Egg yolk	1	1	1
Salt and pepper			
Chopped fresh parsley to garnish			

1. Peel the marrow, cut off one end and scoop out the seeds.

2. Mix the rice, chicken and spices and use to stuff the marrow, tying back the cut end with fine cotton.

3. Place the marrow in a large saucepan, over the yogurt and simmer gently until the marrow is tender. (It will make its own juice.) When the marrow is cooked, strain off the juice and reserve.

4. Melt the butter in a saucepan, add the flour and stir to form a roux. Remove from the heat, beat in the egg yolk, then stir in the marrow cooking juice.

5. Heat gently, stirring, until thickened. Season to taste with salt and pepper. Pour over the marrow before serving sprinkled with parsley.

LIVER WITH YOGURT AND SHERRY

Serves 4–6

	Metric	Imperial	American
Calves' liver, sliced	700 g	1½ lb	1½ lb
Seasoned flour	4 tbsp	4 tbsp	4 tbsp
Butter or margarine	50 g	2 oz	¼ cup
Plain yogurt	250 ml	8 fl oz	1 cup
Sherry	2 tbsp	2 tbsp	2 tbsp
Salt and pepper			

1. Coat the liver in the seasoned flour.

2. Melt the butter or margarine in a pan and fry the liver for 2 minutes on each side. Add the yogurt, sherry and seasoning.

3. Cook, without boiling, until the liver is tender, stirring continuously.

KIDNEYS À LA TURQUE

Serves 4

	Metric	Imperial	American
Butter or margarine	15 g	½ oz	1 tbsp
Onion, chopped	1	1	1
Lamb kidneys, skinned, halved lengthways and cored	8	8	8
Beef stock	600 ml	1 pint	2½ cups
Plain (all-purpose) flour	1 tbsp	1 tbsp	1 tbsp
Dry sherry	1 tbsp	1 tbsp	1 tbsp
Salt and pepper			
Plain yogurt	120 ml	4 fl oz	½ cup
Boiled rice to serve			
Chopped fresh parsley to garnish	1 tsp	1 tsp	1 tsp

1. Heat the butter or margarine in a pan and sauté the onion for a few minutes until soft.

2. Add the kidneys and cook on both sides for 2 minutes. Place the kidneys and onions in an ovenproof casserole.

3. Thicken the stock with flour, bring to the boil, stirring all the time, add the sherry and seasoning and simmer until thick. Pour into the casserole.

4. Cover and cook in the oven at 275°F/140°C (Gas Mark 1) for 2½ hours. Stir in the yogurt.

5. Pile a mound of boiled rice in the centre of a warmed serving dish and place the kidneys around it. Garnish with parsley and serve with a green salad.

ORANGE PLAICE

This delicious fish dish, fancy enough to be used as a dinner-party starter (appetizer), is also easy enough to make a rather special everyday summer meal, especially if served with a substantial green salad.

Serves 4

	Metric	Imperial	American
Yogurt mayonnaise (see page 21)	150 ml	¼ pint	⅔ cup
Oranges	2	2	2
Small plaice fillets	8	8	8
Bunch of watercress to garnish	1	1	1

1. Prepare the mayonnaise first, preferably the day before as the flavour develops with keeping.

2. Grate the rind of one of the oranges, making sure that no pith is included, and squeeze the juice from one half. Slice the remaining orange. Stir the orange juice and grated rind into the mayonnaise.

3. Remove the dark skin from the plaice fillets and roll up. Place them on a buttered heatproof plate, cover and steam over a saucepan of boiling water for 10–20 minutes (depending on size) until tender. Leave to cool.

4. Arrange the cooled fillets on a serving dish, coat with the mayonnaise and place the orange slices around the edge of the dish. Garnish with watercress.

PLAICE DUXELLES

Serves 4

	Metric	Imperial	American
Small plaice fillets	700 g	1½ lb	1½ lb
Milk			
Butter or margarine	15 g	½ oz	1 tbsp
Plain (all-purpose) flour	15 g	½ oz	2 tbsp
Yogurt mayonnaise (see page 21)	2 tbsp	2 tbsp	2 tbsp
Salt and pepper			
Duxelles			
Soft breadcrumbs	50 g	2 oz	1 cup
Chopped dried marjoram or oregano	½ tsp	½ tsp	½ tsp
Chopped fresh parsley	½ tsp	½ tsp	½ tsp
Grated rind of ½ lemon			
Salt and pepper			
Milk to mix			

1. First make the Duxelles. Mix together all the ingredients, adding enough milk to form a paste.

2. Remove the dark skin from the plaice fillets. Spread the Duxelles mixture generously on the skinned side of each fillet and place on a buttered heatproof dish.

3. Cover the fish with kitchen foil and place over a pan of boiling water. Steam for about 15 minutes until tender. Drain, reserving the fish stock, and keep the fish warm.

4. Make the fish stock up to 300 ml/½ pint/1¼ cups with milk.

5. Melt the butter or margarine in a saucepan and stir in the flour to make a roux. Cook for 1–2 minutes, stirring.

6. Remove from the heat and gradually stir in the fish stock and milk mixture. Bring to the boil and simmer for 3 minutes, stirring continuously, until smooth and thickened. Stir in the mayonnaise and season to taste with salt and pepper.

7. Pour the sauce over the plaice fillets and serve immediately.

KIPPEREE

Serves 2–3

	Metric	Imperial	American
Long-grain rice	100 g	4 oz	½ cup
Kipper (kippered herring) fillets	2	2	2
Butter or margarine	25 g	1 oz	2 tbsp
Plain (all-purpose) flour	25 g	1 oz	¼ cup
Milk	300 ml	½ pint	1¼ cups
Plain yogurt	150 ml	¼ pint	⅔ cup
Hard-boiled (hard-cooked) eggs, chopped	2	2	2
Salt and pepper			

1. Cook the rice in boiling water until tender. Drain well, making sure the grains are separate. Poach the kipper fillets for about 5 minutes until tender. Drain well.

2. Melt the butter or margarine in a saucepan, add the flour and cook for 1 minute, stirring, without browning.

3. Remove from the heat and gradually stir in the milk and yogurt. Bring to the boil, stirring continuously, and cook for 2–3 minutes.

4. Add the chopped egg and then the cooked rice. Season to taste with salt and pepper.

5. Serve the rice topped with the kipper fillets.

COD EN PAPILLOTE

Serves 4

	Metric	Imperial	American
Cod steaks	4	4	4
Butter or margarine	50 g	2 oz	¼ cup
Onion, chopped	1	1	1
Button mushrooms, sliced	225 g	8 oz	2 cups
Tomatoes, peeled and sliced	2	2	2
Salt and pepper			
Plain yogurt	4 tbsp	4 tbsp	4 tbsp
Pinch of chopped thyme			

1. Cut four pieces of kitchen foil, each large enough to 'parcel' up a single cod steak, and grease generously on one side with butter or margarine. Lay a cod steak on each greased piece of foil.

2. Heat the remaining butter or margarine in a frying-pan (skillet) and sauté the chopped onion for 2–3 minutes. Add the mushrooms and fry for a further minute.

3. Cover the fish with the onion and mushroom mixture, adding a quarter of the tomato slices, seasoning and 1 tbsp yogurt to each. Sprinkle with thyme.

4. Bring the edges of the foil together and fold it over along all edges to make loose parcels.

5. Place on a baking sheet and bake in the oven at 375°F/190°C (Gas Mark 5) for about 35 minutes. Unwrap and serve.

RUSSIAN HADDOCK

Serves 4

	Metric	Imperial	American
Haddock fillets	450 g	1 lb	1 lb
Seasoned flour	2 tbsp	2 tbsp	2 tbsp
Butter or margarine	100 g	4 oz	1/2 cup
Mushrooms, sliced	100 g	4 oz	1 cup
Plain (all-purpose) flour	50 g	2 oz	1/2 cup
Plain yogurt	250 ml	8 fl oz	1 cup
Salt and pepper			
Hard-boiled (hard-cooked) eggs, sliced	2	2	2
Cheddar cheese, grated	25 g	1 oz	1/4 cup

Garnish
Chopped fresh parsley
Tomato slices
Lemon slices

1. Cut the fish in small slices, coat with seasoned flour and fry in butter or margarine for 10 minutes. Remove from the pan and drain.

2. Fry the mushrooms in the same fat until soft. Stir in the plain flour and add the yogurt gradually, stirring continuously. Season to taste with salt and pepper and heat right through.

3. Layer the fish and egg slices in a shallow heatproof dish and pour the sauce over. Sprinkle with grated cheese and brown under a hot grill (broiler). Garnish with parsley, sliced tomato and lemon slices.

HADDOCK QUICHE

Serves 4

	Metric	Imperial	American
Shortcrust pastry (basic pie dough), thawed if frozen	*225 g*	*8 oz*	*½ lb*
Smoked haddock fillets	*225 g*	*8 oz*	*½ lb*
Butter	*25 g*	*1 oz*	*2 tbsp*
Button mushrooms, sliced	*50 g*	*2 oz*	*½ cup*
Eggs	*2*	*2*	*2*
Milk	*2 tbsp*	*2 tbsp*	*2 tbsp*
Yogurt cheese (see page 11)	*100 g*	*4 oz*	*½ cup*
Juice of 1 lemon			
Salt and pepper			

1. Roll out the pastry and use to line a 20 cm/8 inch flan tin (pan). Prick the bottom with a fork, line with foil or greaseproof (waxed) paper weighted down with baking beans, and bake blind at 400°F/200°C (Gas Mark 6) for 10–15 minutes. Remove foil and beans and bake for a further 5 minutes.

2. Poach the haddock in a little water for 5–10 minutes. Drain, skin and flake. Melt the butter in a frying-pan (skillet) and sauté the mushroom slices. Drain.

3. Beat together the eggs, milk, yogurt cheese and lemon juice. Season to taste with salt and pepper.

4. Fill the flan case (pie shell) with haddock and mushrooms and pour over the egg mixture. Bake in the oven at 400°F/200°C (Gas Mark 6) for about 30 minutes until set and golden. Serve hot or cold.

TUNA FISH CASSEROLE WITH CASHEW NUTS

Serves 4

	Metric	Imperial	American
Can of tuna, drained	198 g	7 oz	7 oz
Butter or margarine	50 g	2 oz	¼ cup
Chopped spring onions (scallions) or chopped chives	1 tbsp	1 tbsp	1 tbsp
Head of celery, chopped	½	½	½
Small can of mushroom soup	1	1	1
Plain yogurt	250 ml	8 fl oz	1 cup
Chinese noodles			
Cashew nuts, whole or chopped	100 g	4 oz	1 cup

1. Break the tuna fish in chunks with a fork.

2. Heat the butter or margarine in a frying-pan (skillet) and sauté the onions or chives and celery for about 5 minutes until soft.

3. Add the mushroom soup, tuna and yogurt, mix together and transfer to an ovenproof casserole. Cover and cook in the oven at 350°F/180°C (Gas Mark 4) for 30 minutes.

4. Meanwhile, cook the noodles in boiling salted water for about 5 minutes until half cooked. Drain well.

5. Spread the noodles over the fish mixture and sprinkle with cashews. Reduce the oven temperature to 325°F/170°C (Gas Mark 3) and cook the casserole for a further 15 minutes.

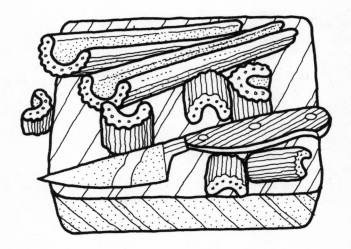

CREAMY CRAB PANCAKES

Serves 8

	Metric	Imperial	American
White fish (e.g. haddock, cod, etc.)	175 g	6 oz	6 oz
Onion	1/2	1/2	1/2
Bay leaf	1	1	1
Butter	25 g	1 oz	2 tbsp
Plain (all-purpose) flour	25 g	1 oz	1/4 cup
Salt and pepper			
Yogurt cheese (see page 11)	100 g	4 oz	1/2 cup
Crabmeat (fresh or canned)			
Pancakes (see page 108)	8	8	8

Garnish
Chopped fresh parsley
Paprika

1. Place the fish in a saucepan with the onion and bay leaf. Cover with water and poach for about 10 minutes, until the fish will flake. Strain, reserving the stock, and flake the fish with a fork.

2. Melt the butter in a saucepan and stir in the flour. Cook for about 2 minutes, stirring, then remove from the heat and gradually stir in the reserved fish stock. Bring to the boil and cook, stirring, until thickened. Season to taste with salt and pepper.

3. Break 75 g/3 oz/1/3 cup yogurt cheese into small pieces and add it, piece by piece, to the sauce, beating all the time. Stir in the flaked fish and crabmeat, taste and adjust seasoning if necessary.

4. Fill the pancakes with the fish mixture and roll up. Spread them with the remaining yogurt cheese and sprinkle with parsley and paprika.

TUNA AND CUCUMBER FLAN

Serves 4

	Metric	Imperial	American
Shortcrust pastry (basic pie dough), thawed if frozen	225 g	8 oz	1/2 lb
Can of tuna, drained and flaked	198 g	7 oz	7 oz
Small cucumber, diced	1/2	1/2	1/2
Yogurt mayonnaise (see page 21)	4 tbsp	4 tbsp	4 tbsp
Plain yogurt	120 ml	4 fl oz	1/2 cup
Salt and pepper			
Apple cider vinegar	2 tsp	2 tsp	2 tsp
Powdered (unflavored) gelatine	3 tsp	3 tsp	3 tsp

1. Roll out the pastry and use to line a 19 cm/7 inch flan tin (pan). Prick the bottom with a fork, line with foil or greaseproof (waxed) paper weighted down with baking beans, and bake blind at 400°F/200°C (Gas Mark 6) for 10–15 minutes. Remove foil and beans and bake for a further 15 minutes until the pastry is firm and golden. Leave to cool.

2. Mix together the mayonnaise and yogurt and stir in the tuna and cucumber. Season to taste with salt and pepper. Spoon into the cooled flan case (pie shell).

3. Stir the vinegar into a little hot water in a small bowl, sprinkle in the gelatine and stir briskly to dissolve. As the gelatine begins to set, pour it over the filled flan. Chill in the refrigerator until set.

4

SALADS AND VEGETABLES

CHICKEN SALAD

Serves 4

	Metric	Imperial	American
Cooked chicken, diced	450 g	1 lb	2 cups
Eating apples, cored and diced	2	2	2
Stick of celery, chopped	1	1	1
Gherkins, chopped	3	3	3
Salt and pepper			
Yogurt mayonnaise (see page 21)	150 ml	1/4 pint	2/3 cup
Hard-boiled (hard-cooked) eggs, sliced	3	3	3
Chopped chives	1 tsp	1 tsp	1 tsp
Lettuce to serve			

1. Mix the diced chicken, apples, celery and gherkins. Season to taste with salt and pepper and moisten with mayonnaise.

2. Top with slices of egg and chopped chives. Serve with lettuce and boiled new potatoes.

STUFFED PEPPERS

Serves 4

	Metric	Imperial	American
Large green peppers	*4*	*4*	*4*
Stuffing			
Minced (ground) cooked chicken	*100 g*	*4 oz*	*½ cup*
Minced (ground) cooked ham	*100 g*	*4 oz*	*½ cup*
Onion, minced (ground)	*1*	*1*	*1*
Mushrooms, finely chopped	*50 g*	*2 oz*	*½ cup*
Salt and pepper			
Good pinch of oregano			
Chicken stock to moisten			
Topping			
Plain yogurt	*150 ml*	*¼ pint*	*⅔ cup*
Egg	*1*	*1*	*1*
Prepared English mustard	*1 tsp*	*1 tsp*	*1 tsp*
Garnish			
Parsley sprigs or paprika			

1. Cut off the stem end from each pepper and remove the core and seeds. Drop the peppers in boiling water and leave for 10 minutes. Drain and cool immediately under cold running water.

2. To make the stuffing, combine all the ingredients, adding enough stock to make a stiff mixture. Use to stuff the peppers tightly.

3. Stand the peppers in a greased ovenproof dish and bake in the oven at 375°F/190°C (Gas Mark 5) for 45 minutes.

4. For the topping, beat together the yogurt, egg and mustard and spoon over the peppers. Cook for a further 20 minutes, or until the topping is set.

5. Garnish with sprigs of parsley and/or a sprinkling of paprika.

SMOKED HADDOCK SALAD

Serves 4

	Metric	Imperial	American
Cooked smoked haddock	225 g	8 oz	1 cup
Cucumber	1/2	1/2	1/2
Eating apples	2	2	2
Lemon juice	1 tbsp	1 tbsp	1 tbsp
Yogurt mayonnaise (see page 21)	150 ml	1/4 pint	2/3 cup
Plain yogurt	150 ml	1/4 pint	2/3 cup
Pinch of curry powder			
Salt and pepper			
Lettuce to serve			

Garnish
Cucumber peel
Lemon slices

1. Skin and flake the fish. Dice the cucumber and core and dice the apples. Sprinkle with lemon juice.

2. Combine all the ingredients and season to taste with salt and pepper. Serve with lettuce and garnish with decoratively cut pieces of cucumber peel and lemon slices.

SALAD CAPRI

Serves 4

	Metric	Imperial	American
Long-grain rice	175 g	6 oz	¾ cup
Green pepper, cored and seeded	1	1	1
Large tomatoes	4	4	4
Prawns (shrimp) in shell	600 ml	1 pint	2 cups
Small can of sweetcorn (whole kernel corn), drained			
Vinaigrette dressing (see page 20)			
Salt and pepper			

1. Cook the rice in boiling water, drain, rinse and cool.

2. Place the pepper in a pan, cover with water, bring to the boil and simmer for 5 minutes. Drain, cool and cut in strips.

3. Cover the tomatoes with boiling water and leave for 1 minute. Drain, peel and cut in slices.

4. Shell the prawns, saving five or six with their shells on for garnish. Pour over the vinaigrette dressing and add all the other ingredients. Mix well and season to taste with salt and pepper. Pile on a serving dish and garnish with the reserved prawns. (Alternatively, make a bed of rice on a rectangular dish and layer the ingredients in strips on top, sprinkling liberally with dressing.)

SPINACH SALAD

Serves 4

	Metric	Imperial	American
Spinach, washed and dried	*450 g*	*1 lb*	*1 lb*
Onion, sliced	*1*	*1*	*1*
Stick of celery, diced	*1*	*1*	*1*
Hard-boiled (hard-cooked) eggs, chopped	*4*	*4*	*4*
Salt and pepper			
Yogurt mayonnaise (see page 21)	*175 ml*	*6 fl oz*	*¾ cup*
Plain yogurt	*175 ml*	*6 fl oz*	*¾ cup*
Pinch of garlic salt			

1. Tear the spinach leaves in small pieces and place in a salad bowl. Add the onion, celery and eggs. Sprinkle with salt and pepper.

2. Dilute the mayonnaise with the yogurt, adding the garlic salt. Pour the mayonnaise over the salad.

Variation
Yogurt cheese (see page 11), broken into chunks, makes a very welcome addition to this salad.

SIDE SALADS

Orange and Watercress Salad

Peel oranges and remove the pith. Slice across thinly with a sharp knife and lay the slices on a long dish, overlapping them slightly. Garnish lavishly with carefully washed and trimmed watercress and sprinkle liberally with a dressing of lemon juice and honey.

(Note: Vinegar should never be used with watercress as it makes it quite indigestible for some people.)

Cucumber Salad

Chill a cucumber, score along its length with a fork and cut in slices. Serve with vinaigrette dressing (see page 20) and sprinkle with finely chopped chives and fresh dill, or a sprinkling of dill seed.

Tomato and Basil Salad

Slice tomatoes thinly with a very sharp knife and lay the slices on a long dish, overlapping them slightly. Sprinkle with basil (fresh if possible, in which case it should be finely chopped) and with freshly milled black pepper. Sprinkle with vinegar.

Pineapple Salad

Shred half a white cabbage. Core, peel and chop a cooking (tart) apple. Dice a stick of celery. Mix all together and add a drained can of pineapple chunks (or use fresh pineapple). Coat with yogurt mayonnaise (see page 21). Serve on lettuce leaves, garnishing with a few halved pineapple chunks or fresh pineapple slivers.

Potato Salad

Boil potatoes in their jackets until just cooked; peel and dice. Finely chop an onion, add to the diced potatoes and coat with yogurt mayonnaise (see page 21), adding a little salt. Garnish with chopped fresh parsley and paprika.

TUNA AND BEAN SALAD

Serves 4

	Metric	Imperial	American
Can of tuna, drained	198 g	7 oz	7 oz
Can of butter (cannellini) beans, drained	425 g	15 oz	15 oz
Spring onions (scallions), thinly sliced	4	4	4
Vinaigrette dressing (see page 20)	3 tbsp	3 tbsp	3 tbsp
Salt and pepper			
Lettuce to serve			

1. Divide the tuna fish into chunks with a fork. Add to the beans and onions and mix well.

2. Moisten with the vinaigrette dressing and season to taste with salt and pepper.

3. Serve on a bed of lettuce or other green salad of your choice.

POLISH BEETROOT

Serves 4–6

	Metric	Imperial	American
Butter or margarine	1 tbsp	1 tbsp	1 tbsp
Onion, chopped	50 g	2 oz	1/2 cup
Plain (all-purpose) flour	1 tbsp	1 tbsp	1 tbsp
Milk	4 tbsp	4 tbsp	4 tbsp
Cooked beetroot (beet), grated	900 g	2 lb	2 lb
Grated horseradish	1 tsp	1 tsp	1 tsp
Salt and pepper			
Pinch of sugar			
Vinegar	1 tbsp	1 tbsp	1 tbsp
Yogurt mayonnaise (see page 21) or plain yogurt	2 tbsp	2 tbsp	2 tbsp

1. Heat the butter or margarine in a pan and sauté the onion for about 5 minutes until soft.

2. Add the flour and cook, stirring, until slightly brown. Remove from the heat and gradually add the milk, stirring continuously. Bring to the boil, stirring.

3. Add the remaining ingredients, except the mayonnaise or yogurt, and simmer for about 6 minutes.

4. Pour into a warmed serving dish and top with the yogurt mayonnaise or plain yogurt.

FRENCH BEANS WITH PEARS

Serves 6

	Metric	Imperial	American
Cooking pears, peeled, cored and thickly sliced	700 g	1½ lb	1½ lb
Boiling chicken stock	450 ml	¾ pint	2 cups
Small piece of lemon peel			
French (green) beans, sliced	450 g	1 lb	1 lb
Streaky (fat) bacon rashers (slices), derinded and diced	4	4	4
Honey	1 tbsp	1 tbsp	1 tbsp
Plain yogurt	1 tbsp	1 tbsp	1 tbsp
Salt and pepper			

1. Drop the pear slices into the saucepan of boiling stock with the lemon peel and simmer for 20 minutes. Add the beans and cook for a further 20 minutes.

2. Place the bacon in a frying-pan (skillet) and fry gently in its own fat until crisp. Remove from the pan with a slotted spoon and stir the honey into the bacon fat. Cook for a few minutes, then add the yogurt and a little of the boiling stock from the saucepan.

3. Mix well, then stir into the pear and bean mixture. Continue cooking, uncovered, until the liquid is reduced and the pears tender. Season to taste with salt and pepper.

4. Serve on individual plates. Sprinkle with black pepper and scatter crisp bacon pieces over the top.

CABBAGE WITH YOGURT AND CARAWAY

Serves 4

	Metric	Imperial	American
Cabbage, shredded	450 g	1 lb	1 lb
Few caraway seeds			
Plain yogurt	150 ml	1/4 pint	2/3 cup

1. Cook the cabbage in the minimum of boiling salted water for about 5 minutes until just tender. Drain well.

2. Stir the caraway seeds into the yogurt and pour over the cabbage. Toss together before serving.

BROCCOLI IN YOGURT SAUCE

Serves 4

	Metric	Imperial	American
Broccoli	450 g	1 lb	1 lb
Plain yogurt	150 ml	¼ pint	⅔ cup
Prepared mustard	1 tsp	1 tsp	1 tsp
Salt and pepper			

1. Cook the broccoli in a pan of boiling salted water for 5–8 minutes until just tender.

2. Mix the yogurt with the mustard and season to taste with salt and pepper.

3. Drain the broccoli well, transfer to a serving dish and pour the yogurt sauce over.

BROAD BEANS À LA TURQUE

This dish is best made with fresh or frozen broad (lima) beans, but can be made with the dried variety if they are well soaked overnight beforehand. Served with rice, it is virtually a meal on its own. It also goes well with fish.

Serves 4

	Metric	Imperial	American
Broad (lima) beans, fresh or frozen	450 g	1 lb	1 lb
Plain yogurt	175 ml	6 fl oz	¾ cup
Garlic clove, crushed	1	1	1
Butter or margarine	15 g	½ oz	1 tbsp
Salt and pepper			
Egg yolk	1	1	1

1. Shell the beans, if necessary, and cook in a pan of boiling salted water for 10–15 minutes until just tender. Drain and put in a heavy saucepan with the yogurt, garlic, butter or margarine and salt and pepper to taste.

2. Warm through, stirring constantly. Add the egg yolk and continue heating gently and stirring until the mixture thickens.

3. Serve with rice or as an accompaniment to fish.

JACKET POTATOES

Serves 4

	Metric	Imperial	American
Large potatoes	4	4	4
Chopped chives	1 tbsp	1 tbsp	1 tbsp
Plain yogurt	4 tbsp	4 tbsp	4 tbsp
Salt and pepper			
Paprika			

1. Scrub and dry the potatoes and bake in the oven at 375°F/190°C (Gas Mark 5) for about 1 hour (depending on size) until they feel soft inside when squeezed.

2. Add the chives to the yogurt and season to taste with salt and pepper.

3. When the potatoes are cooked, put each in a cloth and squeeze until the potato splits open (cutting makes the potato waxy). Spoon in the yogurt mixture and sprinkle with paprika.

5
CAKES AND DESSERTS

CHOCOLATE HONEY COOKIES

Serves 4

	Metric	Imperial	American
Clear honey	2 tsp	2 tsp	2 tsp
Butter or block margarine	225 g	8 oz	1 cup
Chocolate spread	6 tbsp	6 tbsp	6 tbsp
Semi-sweet biscuits, crushed	225 g	8 oz	½ lb
Icing (confectioners') sugar	100 g	4 oz	1 cup

1. Place the honey, butter or margarine and chocolate spread in a saucepan and heat until well melted, stirring all the time. Add the crushed biscuits and mix well until smooth.

2. Pour the mixture into a greased shallow tin (pan) and leave to set. Mix the icing sugar with about 1 tbsp warm water to make glacé icing.

3. When the cookie mixture is cool, cut it into bars or shapes and decorate with glacé icing as liked.

MOCKEROONS

These biscuits contain almond essence and taste very much like macaroons, though the texture is coarser. If you omit the almond essence and add vanilla essence they will be more like flapjacks.

Makes 24

	Metric	Imperial	American
Butter or margarine	75 g	3 oz	6 tbsp
Brown sugar	1 tbsp	1 tbsp	1 tbsp
Clear honey	1½ tbsp	1½ tbsp	1½ tbsp
Few drops of almond essence			
Self-raising flour	100 g	4 oz	1 cup
Rolled oats	225 g	8 oz	2 cups

1. Beat together the butter or margarine, sugar, honey and almond essence until smooth and creamy.

2. Work in the dry ingredients and form the mixture into a roll. Cut across in 24 slices, shape each slice into a ball and flatten slightly between the palms of your hands. Place on two greased baking sheets.

3. Bake in the oven at 375°F/190°C (Gas Mark 5) for 15–20 minutes.

HONEY GINGER CAKE

Makes one 18 cm/7 inch cake

	Metric	Imperial	American
Butter or margarine	100 g	4 oz	½ cup
Soft brown sugar	50 g	2 oz	¼ cup
Clear honey	100 g	4 oz	⅓ cup
Eggs, beaten	2	2	2
Lemon juice	1 tbsp	1 tbsp	1 tbsp
Self-raising flour	225 g	8 oz	2 cups
Pinch of salt			
Ground ginger	1–2 tsp	1–2 tsp	1–2 tsp

Decoration
Glacé icing
Chopped preserved ginger

1. Cream together the butter or margarine and sugar. Beat in the honey, a little at a time, then gradually add the eggs and lemon juice.

2. Sift together the flour, salt and ground ginger and fold into the creamed mixture.

3. Pour the mixture into a greased 18 cm/7 inch cake tin (pan) and cover with a piece of greaseproof (waxed) paper. Bake in the oven at 350°F/180°C (Gas Mark 4) for about 1 hour.

4. Turn out carefully onto a wire rack and leave to cool. Top with glacé icing and decorate with chopped preserved ginger.

WITCHCRAFT CAKE

Serves 6–8

	Metric	Imperial	American
Can of stoned (pitted) black cherries	425 g	15 oz	15 oz
Cornflour (cornstarch)	1 tsp	1 tsp	1 tsp
Chocolate sponge cake	20 cm	8 inch	8 inch
Kirsch	2 tbsp	2 tbsp	2 tbsp
Plain yogurt, whipped	175 ml	6 fl oz	¾ cup
Chocolate curls to decorate			

1. Drain the cherries, reserving the juice. Blend the cornflour with a little of the cherry juice in a saucepan and add the remaining juice. Warm gently, stirring, until thickened, then add the cherries. Allow to cool.

2. Split the cake horizontally and sprinkle both layers with Kirsch.

3. Spread half the whipped yogurt on the bottom layer, cover with the other layer and spoon the cherries over the top.

4. Decorate with the remaining whipped yogurt and the chocolate curls.

HONEY FRUIT BREAD

Makes one 900 g/2 lb loaf

	Metric	Imperial	American
Butter or margarine	225 g	8 oz	1 cup
Soft brown sugar	175 g	6 oz	1 cup
Eggs	4	4	4
Self-raising flour	450 g	1 lb	4 cups
Ground mixed spice (ground allspice)	1 tsp	1 tsp	1 tsp
Ground ginger	1 tsp	1 tsp	1 tsp
Small bananas, mashed	4	4	4
Clear honey	3 tbsp	3 tbsp	3 tbsp
Dates, stoned (pitted) and chopped	100 g	4 oz	1/2 cup
Glacé (candied) cherries, chopped	100 g	4 oz	1/2 cup
Raisins	100 g	4 oz	1/2 cup
Walnuts, chopped	100 g	4 oz	1 cup
Warmed honey to glaze			

1. Cream the butter or margarine with the sugar and beat in the eggs.

2. Sift together the flour, spice and ginger and fold into the creamed mixture, alternating with the mashed bananas and honey. Stir in the fruit and nuts.

3. Spoon into a well greased 900 g/2 lb loaf tin (pan). Bake in the oven at 350°F/180°C (Gas Mark 4) for about 1 hour, covering with greaseproof (waxed) paper if the bread browns too quickly on top.

4. Turn out onto a wire rack and brush the top with warmed honey. Leave to cool.

5. Leave for a day or two before slicing. Serve plain or buttered.

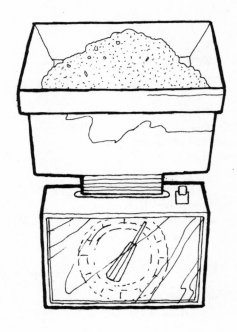

BATTERED BANANAS

Serves 4

	Metric	Imperial	American
Plain (all-purpose) flour	75 g	3 oz	¾ cup
Pinch of salt			
Egg, beaten	1	1	1
Bananas	4	4	4
Clear honey	6 tbsp	6 tbsp	6 tbsp
Oil for deep frying			
Plain yogurt, whipped, to serve			

1. Place the flour and salt in a bowl and make a well in the centre. Add the egg and 4 tbsp water and mix to a thick batter. Gradually add a further 4 tbsp water, beating all the time, until a good coating consistency is formed.

2. Peel the bananas and halve lengthways. Place the honey in a small saucepan with a little water and heat gently to form a syrup. Keep warm.

3. Heat the oil in a deep frying-pan. Dip each piece of banana in batter, then fry in the hot oil until golden. Drain well on kitchen paper towels, then serve with hot syrup poured over. Serve with whipped yogurt.

BAKED APPLES

Serves 4

	Metric	Imperial	American
Medium cooking (tart) apples, cored	4	4	4
Clear honey	2 tbsp	2 tbsp	2 tbsp
Chopped dates	4 tbsp	4 tbsp	4 tbsp
Butter or margarine	15 g	1/2 oz	1 tbsp

1. Make a cut in the skin round the middle of each apple and stand them in a greased baking tin (pan). Pour about 4 tbsp water into the tin.

2. Stuff the apples with a mixture of honey and chopped dates and top each apple with a small knob of butter or margarine.

3. Bake in the oven at 400°F/200°C (Gas Mark 6) for 30–45 minutes until the apples are soft.

Variation
Use raisins or chopped preserved ginger as an alternative to chopped dates.

INDIAN CARROT PUDDING

This is a very sweet pudding and you may like to adjust the amount of honey used. Traditionally, it is served with a decorative piece of silver paper (a star, perhaps) in the centre.

Serves 4

	Metric	Imperial	American
Young carrots	450 g	1 lb	1 lb
Milk	300 ml	½ pint	1¼ cups
Clear honey	2–3 tbsp	2–3 tbsp	2–3 tbsp
Butter or margarine	50 g	2 oz	¼ cup
Pinch of ground cardamom			
Plain yogurt to serve	4 tbsp	4 tbsp	4 tbsp

1. Grate the carrots coarsely, across the grater so that the pieces are short. Place in a small pan with the milk and honey.

2. Simmer very gently, uncovered, for 1½ hours or until all the milk has been absorbed. Stir the mixture occasionally.

3. Add the butter or margarine and cardamom and cook again until they have been absorbed. The carrots will darken and become transparent, but should not be allowed to brown.

4. Serve hot with yogurt, whipped if liked.

FLAT BREAD

Serves 4

	Metric	Imperial	American
Wholewheat flour	225 g	8 oz	2 cups
Butter or margarine, diced	50 g	2 oz	¼ cup
Plain yogurt	250 ml	8 fl oz	1 cup
Clear honey	1 tbsp	1 tbsp	1 tbsp
Salt	1 tsp	1 tsp	1 tsp
Oil for deep frying			

1. Place the flour in a bowl and rub (cut) in the butter or margarine until the mixture resembles breadcrumbs.

2. Blend in the yogurt, honey and salt and knead vigorously. Roll small pieces of dough into balls, then flatten out each ball with a rolling pin.

3. Heat the oil in a deep frying-pan and drop in each piece of bread dough. Cook until puffed up like poppadums. Serve with curry.

APPLE RATAFIA

Serves 4–6

	Metric	Imperial	American
Cooking (tart) apples	450 g	1 lb	1 lb
Clear honey	1 tbsp	1 tbsp	1 tbsp
Egg whites	2	2	2
Caster sugar	100 g	4 oz	1/2 cup
Ratafia biscuits	100 g	4 oz	1 cup
Plain yogurt, whipped	150 ml	1/4 pint	2/3 cup

1. Peel, core and slice the apples. Cook until soft in the minimum of water with the honey.

2. Whisk the egg whites until stiff and whisk in half the sugar. Fold in the remaining sugar and the ratafia biscuits, broken in pieces, reserving six whole biscuits for decoration.

3. Make two piles of the meringue mixture on a sheet of non-stick paper on a baking sheet. Spread into rectangles of equal size.

4. Bake in the coolest possible oven for about 1½ hours until crisp but not coloured. Place, still on the paper, on a wire rack to cool, then carefully peel off the paper.

5. Just before serving, assemble by placing one meringue layer on a serving plate. Spread with the apple and cover with the second meringue layer. Top with whipped yogurt.

HEART OF CREAM

Serves 4

	Metric	Imperial	American
Yogurt cheese (see page 11)	225 g	8 oz	1 cup
Icing (confectioners') sugar	2 tbsp	2 tbsp	2 tbsp
Double (heavy) cream	300 ml	½ pint	1¼ cups
Strawberries, hulled and			
sliced	225 g	8 oz	½ lb
Lemon juice and caster			
(superfine) sugar to serve			

1. Place the yogurt cheese and icing sugar in a blender
   or food processor and blend until smooth. Transfer to
   a bowl, add the cream and whisk until smooth and
   soft.

2. Press the mixture firmly into one large or four small
   heart-shaped moulds and refrigerate overnight.

3. Next day, drain off any liquid from the moulds and turn
   out onto dessert plates. If the moulds still look a little
   moist, blot very carefully with kitchen paper towels.

4. Surround each 'heart' with slices of strawberry and
   sprinkle the fruit with lemon juice and caster sugar
   before serving.

STRAWBERRY SHERBET

1. Use equal quantities of plain yogurt and hulled strawberries.

2. Blend the strawberries to a purée in a blender or food processor.

3. Freeze the yogurt until mushy, then add the strawberry purée and honey to taste.

4. Freeze until mushy again, then turn into a chilled bowl and beat until smooth.

5. Freeze again and remove from the freezer 30 minutes before serving.

Variation
Almost any fruit can be substituted for the strawberries. Fresh apricots are especially good.

BAKED HONEY CUSTARD

Serves 4

	Metric	Imperial	American
Eggs	*3*	*3*	*3*
Milk	*750 ml*	*1¼ pints*	*3 cups*
Clear honey	*3–4 tbsp*	*3–4 tbsp*	*3–4 tbsp*
Vanilla essence	*½ tsp*	*½ tsp*	*½ tsp*

1. Beat the eggs lightly until just mixed, then stir in the other ingredients. Pour into a greased ovenproof dish, or four individual ovenproof ramekins (custard cups). Stand the dish or dishes in a pan with a little water added.

2. Bake in the oven at 350°F/180°C (Gas Mark 4) until the custard sets but is still soft (about 45 minutes-1 hour for a large dish, 30–45 minutes for individual dishes).

3. Serve hot or cold with stewed fruit.

TIPSY YOGURT

Serves 2

	Metric	Imperial	American
Raisins	175 g	6 oz	1 cup
Rum	3 tbsp	3 tbsp	3 tbsp
Plain yogurt	300 ml	½ pint	1¼ cups
Honey to taste			

1. Soak the raisins in the rum overnight.

2. The next day, stir the raisins and rum into the yogurt.

3. Sweeten to taste with honey.

HAZELNUT AND APPLE YOGURT

Serves 4

	Metric	Imperial	American
Eating apples	*2*	*2*	*2*
Lemon juice	*2 tbsp*	*2 tbsp*	*2 tbsp*
Raisins	*1 tbsp*	*1 tbsp*	*1 tbsp*
Hazelnut yogurt (see page 11)	*600 ml*	*1 pint*	*2½ cups*

1. Peel, core and chop the apples and sprinkle them with lemon juice at once to prevent discolouration.

2. Mix the apples and raisins and beat or blend into the hazelnut yogurt.

PANCAKES

Serves 4

	Metric	Imperial	American
Eggs	*4*	*4*	*4*
Milk	*4 tbsp*	*4 tbsp*	*4 tbsp*
Plain yogurt	*250 ml*	*8 fl oz*	*1 cup*
Self-raising flour	*100 g*	*4 oz*	*½ cup*
Salt	*½ tsp*	*½ tsp*	*½ tsp*
Oil for cooking			

1. Beat the eggs and milk until light and fluffy, then gradually add the yogurt, beating constantly.

2. Mix together the flour and salt and gradually beat into the egg mixture. Continue beating until smooth.

3. Heat a little oil in a frying-pan (skillet) and pour off any surplus. Pour in enough pancake batter to cover the bottom of the pan and cook gently until the underside is golden brown. Turn the pancake and cook the second side, then transfer to a plate and keep warm while making the remaining pancakes. Fill as required and serve at once.

Fillings

Orange Pancakes: Fill the pancakes with yogurt (plain or orange-flavoured) and serve with orange sauce: Peel an orange very thinly so that no white pith is included. Cut the peel into matchsticks and add, with the orange juice, to 2 tbsp clear honey and a little water in a saucepan. Bring to the boil and keep warm. Pour over the filled pancakes.

Melba Pancakes: Make Peach Sherbet as for Strawberry Sherbet (page 106) and freeze. Make a sauce by warming raspberry jam with a little arrowroot to thicken, and keep warm. Fill the pancakes with Peach Sherbet, pour over raspberry sauce and serve at once.

Ambrosia Pancakes: Chop walnuts, glacé (candied) cherries and candied peel and fold into whipped plain yogurt. Chill. Warm some clear honey in a little water. Fill the pancakes with the yogurt mixture and pour the honey over.

STRAWBERRIES ANTIGUA

Serves 4

	Metric	Imperial	American
Strawberries, hulled	225 g	8 oz	1/2 lb
Large block of vanilla			
ice-cream			
Caster (superfine) sugar			
Sauce			
Cornflour (cornstarch)	2 tsp	2 tsp	2 tsp
Grated rind and juice of			
1 large orange			
Clear honey	2 tsp	2 tsp	2 tsp
Butter	15 g	1/2 oz	1 tbsp

1. Chill the strawberries in the refrigerator until ready to serve.

2. To make the sauce, blend the cornflour into the orange juice and make up to 150 ml/1/4 pint/2/3 cup with water. Bring to the boil and cook for 3 minutes, stirring continuously. Stir in the honey, orange rind and butter, leave to cool, then chill in the refrigerator.

3. To serve, chill four dessert bowls and place a portion of ice-cream in each one. Top with strawberries and pour over the sauce. Finish with a sprinkling of caster sugar.

APPLE SNOW

Serves 4

	Metric	Imperial	American
Cooking (tart) apples	4	4	4
Caster (superfine) sugar	25 g	1 oz	2 tbsp
Lemon juice	1 tsp	1 tsp	1 tsp
Egg whites	2	2	2
Plain yogurt, whipped, to serve			

1. Core the apples, stand them in a baking tin (pan) and add 4 tbsp water. Bake in the oven at 400°F/200°C (Gas Mark 6) for 45 minutes–1 hour until tender.

2. Scoop the apple pulp out of the skins and press through a sieve, or purée in a blender or food processor. Transfer to a bowl and stir in the sugar and lemon juice.

3. Beat the egg whites until very stiff and fold into the apple purée. Spoon into individual glasses and serve with a generous topping of whipped yogurt.

PAVLOVA

Fillings made with yogurt or yogurt cheese reduce the excess sweetness of this traditional Australian dish.

Serves 4

	Metric	Imperial	American
Egg whites	4	4	4
Caster (superfine) sugar	225 g	8 oz	1 cup
Vanilla essence	1 tsp	1 tsp	1 tsp
Vinegar	1 tsp	1 tsp	1 tsp
Cornflour (cornstarch)	2 tsp	2 tsp	2 tsp

Fillings
See below

1. Draw a 20 cm/8 inch circle on a piece of non-stick baking paper and place it on a baking sheet.

2. Whisk the egg whites until they stand in peaks. Gradually add the sugar, whisking continuously, until very stiff. Continue whisking while gradually adding the vanilla, vinegar and cornflour.

3. Spread two thirds of the meringue mixture over the circle. Spoon the remaining meringue into a piping (pastry) bag, fitted with a large plain nozzle, and pipe a built-up edge round the meringue circle, forming a flat-bottomed meringue 'nest'.

4. Place in the bottom of the oven at 225°F/110°C (Gas Mark ¼) and leave for about 1 hour until the

meringue is dry but not coloured. Cool on a wire rack, then carefully turn over and remove the non-stick lining paper.

5. To serve the pavlova, place the meringue 'nest' on a serving plate and fill with fruit yogurt, such as strawberry or kiwi fruit. Alternatively, serve with a yogurt cheese and fruit filling. Chopped preserved (crystallised) ginger would make a delicious addition. Decorate with slices of fresh fruit.

ORANGES ROMANESQUE

1. Choose nice-looking Jaffa oranges. Cut a small slice from the top of each orange and reserve. Cut away the flesh with the point of a sharp knife so that you are left with empty shells.

2. Remove the membrane from the orange segments and blend the pulp with plain yogurt sweetened with honey. Add a little finely grated orange rind.

3. Freeze the mixture until just mushy, chilling the orange shells at the same time. Spoon the mixture into the shells, replacing the top slice.

4. Chill again before serving.

BAKED YOGURT CHEESECAKE

Serves 6–8

	Metric	Imperial	American
Yogurt cheese (see page 11)	225 g	8 oz	1/2 cup
Caster (superfine) sugar	100 g	4 oz	1/2 cup
Double (heavy) cream	300 ml	1/2 pint	1 1/4 cups
Eggs, separated	3	3	3
Plain (all-purpose) flour	50 g	2 oz	1/2 cup
Grated rind and juice of 1 lemon			
Pastry			
Butter	75 g	3 oz	6 tbsp
Egg, beaten	1	1	1
Plain (all-purpose) flour	175 g	6 oz	1 1/2 cups
Caster (superfine) sugar	1 tsp	1 tsp	1 tsp

1. First make the pastry case (shell). Cream together the butter and beaten egg. Sift in the flour and add the sugar. Mix to a dough and turn out onto a lightly floured surface. Roll out thinly and use to line a greased 23 cm/9 inch round flan tin (pan).

2. To make the filling, whip the yogurt cheese to a thin cream, preferably with a blender or food processor. Add the sugar and cream and whip again until smooth.

3. Beat the egg yolks and one egg white together. Add the flour and grated lemon rind and juice. Beat into the yogurt cheese mixture and continue beating until smooth.

4. Whisk the remaining egg whites until very stiff and fold gently into the mixture.

5. Pour into the pastry case (shell) and bake in the oven at 300°F/150°C (Gas Mark 2) for 1 hour. Turn off the heat and leave the cheesecake in the oven while the oven cools. When cold, chill in the refrigerator until ready to serve.

MELBA COCKTAIL

Serves 4

	Metric	Imperial	American
Fresh peaches, peeled, quartered and stoned (pitted)	4	4	4
Fresh raspberries	175 g	6 oz	1 cup
Large macaroons	3	3	3
Plain yogurt, whipped	120 ml	4 fl oz	½ cup
Caster (superfine) sugar	40 g	1½ oz	3 tbsp

1. Place the peach quarters in the bottom of four sundae glasses. Add a layer of raspberries and leave for 1–2 hours for the juices to mingle.

2. Break the macaroons into pieces and place on top of the raspberries. Top with whipped yogurt and dredge with sugar.

UNBAKED YOGURT CHEESECAKE

Serves 4–6

	Metric	Imperial	American
Yogurt cheese (see page 11)	*175 g*	*6 oz*	*²/₃ cup*
Grated rind and juice of 1 lemon			
Small can of condensed milk			
Biscuit crust			
Digestive biscuits (graham crackers)	*12*	*12*	*12*
Pinch of cinnamon			
Caster (superfine) sugar	*75 g*	*3 oz*	*6 tbsp*
Butter, melted	*100 g*	*4 oz*	*¹/₂ cup*

1. First make the biscuit crust. Crush the biscuits finely in a blender or food processor and mix with the cinnamon, sugar and melted butter. Stir well and press into the base of a greased 20 cm/8 inch round flan tin (pan).

2. To make the filling, beat together the yogurt cheese and grated lemon rind and juice until smooth. Fold in the condensed milk.

3. Pour the filling onto the biscuit base and chill in the refrigerator until set.

Variations
Orange Cheesecake: Substitute the grated rind and juice of one orange for the lemon.

Rum and Raisin Cheesecake: Soak raisins in rum overnight and fold carefully into the cheesecake mixture.

FRUIT MELANGE

Serves 4

	Metric	Imperial	American
Caster (superfine) sugar	1½ tbsp	1½ tbsp	1½ tbsp
Large juicy oranges	3	3	3
Bananas	2	2	2
Toasted shredded coconut	3 tbsp	3 tbsp	3 tbsp
Plain yogurt, whipped	120 ml	4 fl oz	½ cup

1. Place the sugar in a small saucepan with a little water and heat until dissolved. Leave to cool.

2. Squeeze the juice from one orange and add it to the sugar syrup. Peel the remaining two oranges, removing all pith, and cut into slices. Peel and slice the bananas.

3. Arrange the fruit in layers in four sundae dishes. Pour over the sweetened juice and sprinkle with coconut. Top with whipped yogurt and serve at once.

Note
If you make this dessert in advance, dip the banana slices in lemon juice to prevent them discolouring.

PEACHES ROYALE

Serves 4

	Metric	Imperial	American
Fresh peaches	4	4	4
Cointreau	2 tbsp	2 tbsp	2 tbsp
Clear honey	1 tbsp	1 tbsp	1 tbsp
Orange juice	1 tbsp	1 tbsp	1 tbsp

To serve
Savoy or Boudoir biscuits
  (ladyfingers)
Plain yogurt

1. Peel and halve the peaches and remove the stones (pits).

2. Mix the Cointreau, honey and orange juice and pour over the peaches. Chill thoroughly.

3. Serve the peaches with Savoy or Boudoir biscuits (ladyfingers) and thin or whipped yogurt.

Variation
Canned peaches can be used instead of fresh

SWEETS, SPREADS AND DRINKS

HONEY MARZIPAN

Use this unusual but delicious marzipan to make sweets and petits fours, or roll out and use to cover a fruit cake.

Makes about 225 g/8 oz/½ lb

	Metric	Imperial	American
Butter	40 g	1½ oz	3 tbsp
Icing (confectioners') sugar	50 g	2 oz	½ cup
Clear honey	1 tbsp	1 tbsp	1 tbsp
Freshly ground almonds	100 g	4 oz	1 cup
Few drops of vanilla essence			

1. Place the butter, sugar and honey in a saucepan and heat gently to melt. Bring slowly to the boil, stirring, then remove from the heat and leave to cool slightly.

2. Add the ground almonds and vanilla to taste and mix to a stiff paste, adding a little water if necessary. Turn onto a board and knead thoroughly until the marzipan is pliable and free from cracks.

HONEY CURD

Makes about 450 g/1 lb/1 lb

	Metric	Imperial	American
Egg whites	*3*	*3*	*3*
Egg yolks	*4*	*4*	*4*
Clear honey	*300 ml*	*½ pint*	*1¼ cups*
Butter	*225 g*	*8 oz*	*1 cup*
Juice and grated rind of			
* 2 lemons*			

1. Mix all the ingredients together and place in the top of a double saucepan. Cook over very gentle heat until the mixture thickens.

2. Pour immediately into warm jars and seal.

Note:
Stored in a cool place, Honey Curd should keep for at least a year.

HONEY POPCORN

1. The making (and eating) of popcorn is a pleasant pursuit on a rainy day during the school holidays (vacation). If you haven't got a proper popper, use any heavy-based saucepan with a tightly fitting lid. Never try to pop corn in a pan without a lid.

2. The principle is simple: If you subject the corn to sufficient dry heat, the kernels will puff up and burst. Always use the correct 'popping' corn.

3. Boil 450 g/1 lb clear honey until it is very thick. Remove from the heat and add the popped corn. Stir to coat thoroughly. When it is cool enough to handle form into balls.

4. Popcorn balls tied with ribbon make excellent decorations for children's parties or for hanging on the Christmas tree.

HONEY BUTTERSCOTCH

Makes about 700 g/1½ lb/1½ lb

	Metric	Imperial	American
Clear honey	450 g	1 lb	1⅓ cups
Butter, melted	225 g	8 oz	1 cup
Salt	½ tsp	½ tsp	½ tsp
Few drops of vanilla essence			

1. Put the honey in a saucepan and bring to the boil, stirring all the time, until it thickens and a tiny quantity dropped in water will harden instantly. Remove from the heat and stir in the butter, salt and vanilla.

2. Pour the mixture into a well-greased shallow tin (pan) and leave until almost set. Mark into small squares and leave until completely cold. Break up into squares and wrap in greaseproof (waxed) paper.

HONEYCOMB TOFFEE

Makes about 175 g/6 oz/6 oz

	Metric	Imperial	American
Caster (superfine) sugar	50 g	2 oz	¼ cup
Clear honey	100 g	4 oz	⅓ cup
Bicarbonate of soda (baking soda)	1 tsp	1 tsp	1 tsp

1. Place the sugar and honey in a saucepan and bring to the boil. Cook until a deep golden brown. While still boiling, add the bicarbonate of soda, stirring it in very quickly.

2. Pour the mixture into a well-greased shallow tin (pan). When the toffee is almost firm, slide a greased knife round the edges to loosen the toffee from the tin and turn it out onto a wire rack to cool.

3. When the toffee is quite cold, break it into small pieces by tapping with a rolling pin or toffee hammer.

HONEY BUTTER

Makes about 225 g/8 oz/1 cup

	Metric	Imperial	American
Clear honey	*2 tbsp*	*2 tbsp*	*2 tbsp*
Butter or margarine	*225 g*	*8 oz*	*1 cup*

1. Beat together the honey and butter or margarine until light and creamy.

2. Use as a spread on bread, toast and cakes or as a cake filling.

Variations

Lemon or Orange Honey Butter: Beat 1 tbsp lemon or orange juice into the Honey Butter, followed by the grated rind of one lemon or orange.

Spiced Honey Butter: Beat ½ tsp each of ground nutmeg, cinnamon and allspice into the Honey Butter.

Ginger Honey Butter: Beat 1 tbsp chopped crystallized (candied) ginger into the Honey Butter.

HONEY FUDGE

Makes about 700 g/1½ lb/1½ lb

	Metric	Imperial	American
Single (light) cream	*150 ml*	*¼ pint*	*⅔ cup*
Small can of sweetened condensed milk			
Butter or margarine	*100 g*	*4 oz*	*½ cup*
Clear honey	*2 tbsp*	*2 tbsp*	*2 tbsp*
Icing (confectioners') sugar	*450 g*	*1 lb*	*3½ cups*
Pinch of cream of tartar			

1. Mix all the ingredients in a heavy-bottomed saucepan. Bring to the boil slowly, stirring all the time and making sure the ingredients dissolve evenly.

2. Boil rapidly, stirring occasionally for about 8 minutes, until a small amount dropped into a little water forms a soft ball (at 240°F).

3. Remove the pan from the heat, leave to cool slightly, then beat the mixture until thick. Pour into a greased shallow 18 cm/7 inch square tin (pan). Leave until almost set, then mark deeply into small squares.

4. When the fudge is quite set, remove from the tin, break into pieces and place on a wire rack to harden.

Variations
Coffee Fudge: Add 1 tbsp strong coffee, or ½ tsp instant coffee dissolved in ½ tbsp hot water, just before beating the cooked mixture.
Chocolate Fudge: Melt 15 g/½ oz/½ square chocolate and add just before beating the cooked mixture.

COONARDOO

Serves 2

	Metric	Imperial	American
Plain yogurt	600 ml	1 pint	2½ cups
Iced water	300 ml	½ pint	1¼ cups
Salt	½ tsp	½ tsp	½ tsp
Chopped fresh mint	1 tbsp	1 tbsp	1 tbsp
Sprigs of fresh mint	2	2	2

1. Place the yogurt, iced water, salt and chopped mint in a blender or food processor and blend until frothy.

2. Serve in chilled glasses sprinkled with a little extra chopped mint. Place a sprig of mint on the rim of each glass to decorate.

YOGURT SHAKES

1. Use equal quantities of plain yogurt, fresh milk and fruit.

2. Blend in a blender or food processor until smooth.

3. Sweeten to taste with honey and serve chilled.

INDEX